39092066755028
4/9/2008
Nardo, Don,
Words of the ancient Romans
:

The Lucent Library of Historical Eras

Words of the Ancient Romans
Primary Sources

Don Nardo, Editor

LUCENT BOOKS®

THOMSON
GALE

San Diego • Detroit • New York • San Francisco • Cleveland • New Haven, Conn. • Waterville, Maine • London • Munich

Romulus and Remus Nursed by the She-Wolf, by Domenico Corvi.

LIBRARY OF CONGRESS CATALOGING-IN-PUBLICATION DATA

Nardo, Don, 1947–
   Words of the ancient Romans : primary sources / By Don Nardo.
     v. cm. — (The Lucent library of historical eras. Ancient Rome)
Includes bibliographical references and index.
Contents: Rome's founding and early expansion—Julius Caesar's exploits and
conquests—Reign of Augustus, the first emperor—The home and family life—
Entertainment and leisure activities—Gods and religious worship.
   ISBN 1-59018-318-5 (hardback : alk. paper)
   1. Rome—History—Sources—Juvenile literature. [1. Rome—History—Sources.]
I. Title. II. Series.
   DG13.N37 2003
   937—dc21
                                      2003001645

Contents

Foreword

Looking back from the vantage point of the present, history can be viewed as a myriad of intertwining roads paved by human events. Some paths stand out—broad highways whose mileposts, even from a distance of centuries, are clear. The events that propelled the rise to power of Germany's Third Reich, its role in World War II, and its eventual demise, for example, are well defined and documented.

Other roads are less distinct, their route sometimes hidden from view. Modern legislatures may have developed from old tribal councils, for example, but the links between them are indistinct in places, open to discussion and interpretation.

The architecture of civilization—law, religion, art, science, and government—as well as the more everyday aspects of our culture—what we eat, what we wear—all developed along the historical roads and byways. In that progression can be traced every facet of modern life.

A broad look back along these roads reveals that many paths—though of vastly different character—seem to converge at a few critical junctions. These intersections are those great historical eras that echo over the long, steady course of human history, extending beyond the past and into the present.

These epic periods of time are the focus of Lucent's Library of Historical Eras. They shine through the mists of history like beacons, illuminated by a burst of creativity that propels events forward—so bright that we, from thousands of years away, can clearly see the chain of events leading to the present.

Each Lucent Library of Historical Eras consists of a set of books that highlight various aspects of these major eras. For example, the Elizabethan England library features volumes on Queen Elizabeth I and her court, Elizabethan theater, the great playwrights, and everyday life in Elizabethan London.

The mini-library approach allows for the division of each era into its most significant and most interesting parts and the exploration of those parts in depth. Also, social and cultural trends as well as illustrative documents and eyewitness accounts can be prominently featured in individual volumes.

4

Lucent's Library of Historical Eras presents a wealth of information to young readers. The lively narrative, fully documented primary and secondary source quotations, maps, photographs, sidebars, and annotated bibliographies serve as launching points for class discussion and further research.

In studying the great historical eras, students also develop a better understanding of our own times. What we learn from the past and how we apply it in the present may shape the future and may determine whether our era will be a guiding light to those traveling future roads.

Rome's Founding and Early Expansion

The Romans placed great store in traditions, especially those molded in the early, formative years of their realm. In the turbulent years of the waning Republic (the first century B.C., by which time Rome controlled most of the Mediterranean world), most Romans looked back fondly to their early folk heroes. The common belief was that these were bigger-than-life figures; yet they were not big in the wealthy, showy, or arrogant sense. Instead, they were simple, homespun individuals who were concerned more with virtue, personal honor, and duty and service to family and country than with wealth and prestige. Guided by such strength of character, in this view, they took a crude, backward farming community and transformed it into a noble nation and empire.

Though likely based to some degree on real people, these admirable characters from Rome's past were more ideal than real. Yet they helped to shape and define an exemplary national character that the Romans believed they possessed. "The legends of Rome's early heroes," noted scholar Jo-Ann Shelton points out, "articulate this national self-image, and they are instructive because they indicate to us how the Romans perceived of themselves."[1] In fact, the Romans perceived of themselves very much like most modern Americans see themselves—as a just and morally virtuous people destined to create a better world. The first-century historian Livy stated it well in the introduction to his great history of his nation:

I hope my passion for Rome's past has not impaired my judgment; for I do honestly believe that no country has ever been greater or purer than ours or richer in good citizens and noble deeds; none has been free for so many generations from the vices of avarice [greed] and luxury; nowhere have thrift and plain living been for so long held in such esteem. [2]

In examining Rome's founding and phenomenal early expansion, therefore, one must keep in mind the Romans' own national character and self-image. What to the modern eye may appear as arrogance, imperialism, and naked conquest was to them justified, inevitable, and for the greater good of all in the long run. First they defeated and absorbed their Italian neighbors, unifying the peninsula; then they overcame the empire of Carthage (in the three Punic Wars), which controlled the western Mediterranean; finally, they overran the Greek lands in the eastern sector of that sea and turned them into provinces. In the Roman view, this was part of a divine and greater destiny, not unlike the "manifest destiny" that drove the early United States in its acquisition of all the territories lying between the Atlantic and Pacific. Indeed, like the United States at present, Rome was the lone superpower of its day and quite proud of it. "So great is the glory won by the Roman people," Livy said, "that when they declare that Mars [god of war] himself was . . . father of the man who founded their city, all the nations of the world might well allow the claim as readily as they accept Rome's imperial domination." [3]

Notes

1. Jo-Ann Shelton, ed., *As The Romans Did: A Sourcebook in Roman Social History.* New York: Oxford University Press, 1988, p. 4.
2. Livy, *The History of Rome from Its Foundation,* Books 1–5 published as *Livy: The Early History of Rome,* trans. Aubrey de Sélincourt. New York: Penguin, 1960, p. 34.
3. Livy, *History of Rome,* pp. 33–34.

Rome's Destiny Foretold

According to the first-century B.C. *poet Virgil in his great epic, the* Aeneid, *a prince of Troy—Aeneas—escaped that city's destruction, traveled to Italy, and established the Roman race. In this passage, Jupiter, king of the gods, reveals to the love goddess, Venus, how that race will fulfill its destiny to rule the world.*

I shall tell you more, unrolling for you the secrets of the scroll of the Fates. He [Aeneas] will wage a great war in Italy and crush its fierce tribes. He will build walls for his people and establish their way of life, until a third summer has seen him reigning in Latium and a third winter has passed after the subjection of the Rutulians [a warlike Italian race]. But the reign of his son Ascanius, who now receives the second name Iulus . . . shall last while thirty long years revolve, and he shall transfer his kingdom from its seat at Lavinium and build a city with powerful fortifications at Alba Longa. Here the rule of the race of Hector [i.e., the Trojan race] will last for three hundred long years until Ilia the royal priestess, heavy with the seed of Mars, shall give birth to twin sons. Then Romulus shall receive the people, wearing with joy the tawny hide of the wolf which nursed him. The walls he builds will be the walls of Mars and he shall give his own name to his people, the Romans. On them I impose no limits of time or place. I have given them an empire that will know no end. Even angry Juno, who is now wearying sea and land and sky with her terrors, will come to better counsel and join with me in cherishing the people of Rome, the rulers of the world, the race that wears the toga. So it has been decreed.

Virgil, *Aeneid*, trans. David West. New York: Penguin, 1990, pp. 11–12.

Romulus Slays Remus

In his biography of Romulus, founder of Rome, the prolific first-century A.D. Greek writer Plutarch gives this account of the quarrel that led Romulus to kill his brother.

Their minds being full bent upon building, there arose presently a difference about the place. Romulus chose what was called Roma Quadrata, or the Square Rome, and would have the city there. Remus laid out a piece of ground on the Aventine Mount, well fortified by nature, which was from him called Remonium, but now Rignarium. Concluding at last

to decide the contest by a divination from a flight of birds, and placing themselves apart at some distance. Remus, they say, saw six vultures, and Romulus double that number; others say, Remus did truly see his number, and that Romulus feigned his, but when Remus came to him, that then he did indeed see twelve. . . .

When Remus knew the cheat, he was much displeased; and as Romulus was casting up a ditch, where he designed the foundation of the city-wall, he turned some pieces of the work to ridicule, and obstructed others; at last, as he was in contempt leaping over it, some say Romulus himself struck him, others Celer, one of his companions; he fell, however, and in the scuffle Faustulus [the shepherd who had raised the two brothers] also was slain, and Plistinus, who, being Faustulus's brother, story tells us, helped to bring up Romulus. Celer upon this fled instantly into Tuscany, and from him the Romans call all men that are swift of feet Celeres; and because Quintus Metellus, at his father's funeral, in a few days' time gave the people a show of gladiators, admiring his expedition in getting it ready, they gave him the name of Celer.

Romulus, having buried his brother Remus, together with his two foster-fathers, on the mount Remonia, set to building his city.

Plutarch, *Life of Romulus*, in *Parallel Lives*, published complete as *Lives of the Noble Grecians and Romans*, trans. John Dryden. New York: Random House, 1932, pp. 30–31.

Romulus slays his brother Remus in this engraving. Although they are legendary figures, it is possible they are based to some extent on real people.

Early Rome Begins to Grow

In his History of Rome, *the first-century B.C. Roman historian Livy records the legend of Rome's early years, including this passage about initial population growth and the emergence of the noble patrician class, which would remain the most prestigious social group throughout the nation's history.*

Meanwhile Rome was growing. More and more ground was coming within the circuit of its walls. Indeed, the rapid expansion of the enclosed area was out of proportion to the actual population, and evidently indicated an eye to the future. In antiquity the founder of a new settlement, in order to increase its population, would as a matter of course shark up a lot of homeless and destitute folk and pretend that they were 'born of earth' to be his progeny; Romulus now followed a similar course: to help fill his big new town, he threw open, in the ground—now enclosed—between the two copses as you go up the Capitoline hill, a place of asylum for fugitives. Hither fled for refuge all the rag-tag-and-bobtail from the neighbouring peoples: some free, some slaves, and all of them wanting nothing but a fresh start. That mob was the first real addition to the City's strength, the first step to her future greatness.

Having now adequate numbers, Romulus proceeded to temper strength with policy and turned his attention to social organization. He created a hundred senators—fixing that number either because it was enough for his purpose, or because there were no more than a hundred who were in a position to be made 'Fathers', as they were called, or Heads of Clans. The title of 'fathers' (*patres*) undoubtedly was derived from their rank, and their descendants were called 'patricians'.

Livy, *The History of Rome from Its Foundation*, Books 1–5 published as *Livy: The Early History of Rome*, trans. Aubrey de Sélincourt. New York: Penguin, 1960, pp. 42–43.

Establishment of the Republic

According to legend, the son of Rome's last king, Tarquinius Superbus, raped Lucretia, daughter of a Roman nobleman. This touched off a revolution that ousted the Tarquin family (or Tarquinii) and established the Roman Republic in 509 B.C. In this account by the first-century B.C. Greek historian Dionysius of Halicarnassus, the leader of the revolution,

Lucius Junius Brutus, rallies the people and helps set up the new government, including the office of consul (administrator-general).

When Brutus had done haranguing [the citizenry assembled in the Forum], they all cried out, as from a single mouth, to lead them to arms. Then Brutus, pleased at this, said, "On this condition, that you first hear the resolution of the senate and confirm it. For we have resolved that the Tarquinii and all their posterity shall be banished both from the city of Rome and from all the territory ruled by the Romans; that no one shall be permitted to say or do anything about their restoration; and that if anyone shall be found doing anything contrary to these decisions he shall be put to death. If it is your pleasure that this resolution be confirmed, divide yourselves into your *curiae* [political wards, ten to each of Rome's original three tribes] and give your votes; and let the exercise of this right be the beginning of your liberty." This was done; and all the *curiae* having given their votes for the banishment of the tyrants, Brutus again came forward and said, "Now that our first measures have been confirmed in the manner required, hear also what we have further resolved concerning the form of our government. It was our decision, upon considering what magistracy [political power] should be in control of affairs, not to establish the kingship again, but to appoint two annual magistrates [the consuls] to hold the royal power, these men to be whomever you yourselves shall choose in the *comitia* [assembly], voting by centuries. If, therefore, this also is your pleasure, give your votes to that effect." The people approved of this resolution likewise, not a single vote being given against it. After that Brutus, coming forward, appointed Spurius Lucretius as *interrex* to preside, according to ancestral custom, over the *comitia* for the election of magistrates. And he, dismissing the assembly, ordered all the people to go promptly in arms to the field [the "Field of Mars," where military troops practiced] where it was their custom to elect their magistrates. When they were come thither, he chose two men to perform the functions which had belonged to kings—Brutus and Collatinus; and the people, being called by centuries, confirmed their appointment. Such were the measures taken in the city at that time.

Dionysius of Halicarnassus, *Roman Antiquities,* quoted in Naphtali Lewis and Meyer Reinhold, eds., *Roman Civilization, Sourcebook I: The Republic.* New York: Harper and Row, 1966, pp. 57–58.

First Battles Against the Greeks

In the years following the founding of the Republic, Rome had little trouble subduing its immediate neighbors. Then it came up against a Greek army commanded by Pyrrhus, king of Epirus, who had landed in Italy in 280 B.C. to help the Greek city of Taras stave off the Romans. Although Pyrrhus won the ensuing battles, the Romans

proved so tough and stubborn he was forced to return to his homeland. This is Plutarch's account of Pyrrhus's first encounter with the Romans.

The news now reached Pyrrhus that Laevinus, the Roman consul, was advancing on the city with a large army, plundering Lucania as he came. Pyrrhus' allies had not yet arrived, but he thought it disgraceful to remain inactive and allow the enemy to advance any nearer, and so he marched out with his troops. He had first dispatched a herald to the Romans to ask whether they would agree to receive satisfaction from the Italian Greeks before resorting to arms, and he offered his services as arbitrator and mediator. Laevinus' reply was that the Romans neither accepted Pyrrhus as a mediator nor feared him as an enemy, whereupon Pyrrhus advanced and pitched his camp in the plain between the cities of Pandosia and Heracleia.

When he discovered that the Romans were close by and had encamped on the other side of the river Siris, he rode up to reconnoitre the position. Their discipline, the arrangement of their watches, their orderly movements and the planning of their camp all impressed and astonished him, and he remarked to the friend nearest him, 'These may be barbarians, but there is nothing barbarous about their discipline'. . . .

Pyrrhus was disturbed by this, so he ordered his infantry officers to take up their battle formation at once and wait under arms, while he himself advanced with his force of three thousand cavalry: he hoped to catch the Romans while they were still engaged in crossing the river and before they could regain their formation. But when he saw the glittering line of shields of the Roman infantry stretching along the bank, while their cavalry advanced against him in good order, he closed up his own ranks and led them in charge. . . .

The Romans resisted their onslaught bravely and for a long while the issue hung in the balance. It is said that the mastery of the field changed hands no less than seven times, as each side gave ground in turn or advanced. The king's change of armour, although well-timed for his personal safety, came near to losing him the battle. Many of the enemy attacked Megacles [who was carrying Pyrrhus's cloak and armor], and the man who first struck him, Decius, seized his cloak and helmet and rode up with them to Laevinus: as he did so he brandished them aloft and shouted out that

The Romans battle Pyrrhus's elephants in 280 B.C. Although the Greeks were victorious, Pyrrhus lost many of his best men in the fighting.

he had killed Pyrrhus. The Romans, when they saw these trophies exultantly displayed and carried along their ranks, shouted aloud in triumph: the Greeks, on the other hand, were disheartened and dejected until Pyrrhus, discovering what had happened, rode along his line with bared head stretching out his hand to his allies and making himself known to them by his voice. At last, as the Romans began to be driven back by the elephants and their horses, before they could get near the great beasts, started to panic and bolt, Pyrrhus seized his opportunity: as the Romans faltered, he launched a charge with his Thessalian cavalry and routed the enemy with great slaughter.

According to Dionysius the Romans lost nearly fifteen thousand men and Pyrrhus thirteen thousand, while Hieronymus reduces these figures to seven thousand on the Roman side and four thousand on the Greek. But these were some of Pyrrhus' best troops, and in addition he lost many of the friends and commanders whom he trusted and employed the most.

Plutarch, *Life of Pyrrhus*, in *The Age of Alexander: Nine Greek Lives by Plutarch*, trans. Ian Scott-Kilvert. New York: Penguin, 1973, pp. 401–403.

Building Rome's First Navy

The Romans faced their toughest foe in their biggest war yet when in 264 B.C. they

Early in the First Punic War, the Romans built warships with three banks of oars, like this galley.

squared off against Carthage in the First Punic War. Rome's great disadvantage was that Carthage was a great sea power, while Rome had no warships. The second-century B.C. *Greek historian Polybius tells how the Romans met the challenge.*

So long as the Carthaginians held unchallenged control of the sea, the issue of the war still hung in the balance. In the months that followed many of the inland cities came over to the Romans for fear of their army now that they were in possession of Agrigentum, but at the same time many of the coastal cities deserted them because they were overawed by the Carthaginian fleet. So when the Romans saw that the balance of advantage continually oscillated from one side to another for this reason, and that while the Italian coasts were repeatedly raided and devastated those of Africa suffered no damage, they were filled with the desire to take to sea and meet the Carthaginians there. It was this factor among others which persuaded me to describe the war at greater length than I would otherwise have done. I was anxious that my readers should not remain ignorant of an important initiative of this kind: that is, how and when and for what reasons the Romans first ventured upon the sea.

It was, therefore, because they saw that the war was dragging on that they first applied themselves to building ships—100 quinqueremes and twenty triremes. They faced great difficulties because their shipwrights were completely inexperienced in the building of a quinquereme, since these vessels had never before been employed in Italy. Yet it is this fact which illustrates better than any other the extraordinary spirit and audacity of the Romans' decision. It was not a question of having adequate resources for the enterprise, for they had in fact none whatsoever, nor had they ever given a thought to the sea before this. But once they had conceived the idea, they embarked on it so boldly that without waiting to gain any experience in naval warfare they immediately engaged the Carthaginians, who had for generations enjoyed an unchallenged supremacy at sea. One piece of evidence of their extraordinary daring, and of the truth of my account, is this. When they first ventured to transport their forces to Messana, not only had they no decked ships, but no warships at all, not so much as a single galley. They merely borrowed penteconters and triremes from the Tarentines, the Locrians and the people of Elea and Neapolis, and ferried the troops across at great risk. It was on this occasion that the Carthaginians sailed out to attack them as they were crossing the straits, and one of their decked ships, in their eagerness to overtake the transports, ventured too near the shore, ran aground, and fell into the hands of the Romans. It was this ship which they proceeded to use as a model, and they built their whole fleet according to its specifications; from which it is clear that but for this accident they would have been prevented from carrying out their programme for sheer lack of the necessary knowledge.

As it was, those who had been given the task of shipbuilding occupied themselves with the construction work, while others collected the crews and began to teach them to row on shore in the following way. They placed the men along the rowers' benches on dry land, seating them in the same order as if they were on those of an actual vessel, and then stationing the *keleustes* [the man who kept the beat for the rowers] in the middle, they trained them to swing back their bodies in unison bringing their hands up to them, then to move forwards again thrusting their hands in front of them, and to begin and end these movements at the *keleustes'* word of command. When the crews had learned this drill, the ships were launched as soon as they were finished.

Polybius, *The Histories,* published as *Polybius: The Rise of the Roman Empire,* trans. Ian Scott-Kilvert. New York: Penguin, 1979, pp. 62–63.

Hannibal's Hatred for Rome

After Rome won the First Punic War, Carthage's great general Hamilcar Barca nurtured a deep contempt for the Romans. As Livy tells it, Hamilcar passed on that hatred to his son, Hannibal, who would go on to cause Rome much trouble.

The intensity of the feeling is illustrated by an anecdote of Hannibal's boyhood: his father Hamilcar, after the campaign in Africa, was about to carry his troops over into Spain, when Hannibal, then about nine years old, begged, with all the childish arts he could muster, to be allowed to accompany him; whereupon Hamilcar, who was preparing to offer sacrifice for a

Young Hannibal, standing before an altar with his father, Hamilcar Barca, swears everlasting hatred for Rome. This vow eventually proved ruinous to both Hannibal and Carthage.

successful outcome, led the boy to the altar and made him solemnly swear, with his hand upon the sacred victim, that as soon as he was old enough he would be the enemy of the Roman people. Hamilcar was a proud man and the loss of Sicily and Sardinia was a cruel blow to his pride; he remembered, moreover, that Sicily had been surrendered too soon, before the situation had become really desperate, and that Rome, taking advantage of internal troubles in Africa, had tricked Carthage into the loss of Sardinia, and then had added insult to injury by the imposition of a tribute. All this rankled in his mind, and his conduct of affairs during the five years of the war in Africa, following hard upon the signature of peace with Rome, and subsequently during the nine years he spent in extending Carthaginian influence in Spain, made it clear enough that his ultimate object was an enterprise of far greater moment, and that if he had lived the invasion of Italy would have taken place under Hamilcar's leadership, instead of, as actually happened, under Hannibal's.

Livy, *The History of Rome from Its Foundation*, Books 21–30 published as *Livy: The War with Hannibal*, trans. Aubrey de Sélincourt. New York: Penguin, 1972, pp. 23–24.

Hannibal Crosses the Alps

As the Second Punic War commenced in 218 B.C., Hannibal surprised the Romans by leading his army through the Alps and into the Po Valley in northern Italy. Polybius gives this account of some of the obstacles the Carthaginians encountered.

Hannibal saw that his men had lost heart because of the sufferings they had already endured and the hardships which they believed still lay ahead. So he called his troops together and strove to raise their spirits, and for this purpose he relied above all on the actual sight of Italy, which now stretched out before them, for the country lies so close under these mountains that when the two are seen simultaneously in a panoramic view, the Alps seem to rise above the rest of the landscape, like a walled citadel above a city. Hannibal therefore directed his men's gaze towards the plains of the Po, and reminded them of the welcome they would receive from the Gauls who inhabited them. At the same time he pointed out the direction of Rome itself, and in this way he did something to restore their confidence. The next day he broke camp and began the descent. During this part of his march he met none of the enemy except for a few prowling marauders, but because of the snow and of the dangers of his route he lost nearly as many men as he had done on the ascent. The track which led down the mountainside was both narrow and steep, and since neither the men nor the animals could be sure of their footing on account of the snow, any who stepped wide of the path or stumbled overbalanced and fell down the precipices. These perils they could endure, because by this time they had become

Hannibal watches his army wind its way through a treacherous Alpine pass. Thousands of men and animals died along the way.

accustomed to such mischances, but at length they reached a place where the track was too narrow for the elephants or even the pack animals to pass. A previous landslide had already carried away some 300 yards of the face of the mountain, while a recent one had made the situation still worse. At this point the soldiers once more lost their nerve and came close to

despair. Hannibal's first thought was to avoid this impasse by making a detour, but a fresh fall of snow made further progress impossible and he was compelled to abandon the idea.

These conditions were so unusual as to be almost freakish. The new snow lying on top of the old, which had remained there from the previous winter, gave way easily, both because it was soft, having only just fallen, and because it was not yet deep. But when men and beasts had trodden through it and penetrated to the frozen snow underneath, they no longer sank into it, but found both their feet slipping from under them, as happens when people walk on ground which is covered with a coating of mud. What followed made the situation even more desperate. In the case of the men, when they found they could not get a foothold on the lower layer of snow, they fell, and then, as they struggled to rise by using their hands and knees, slid downwards even faster on these, no matter what they clutched on the way, since the angle of the slope was so steep.

As for the animals, when they fell and struggled to rise they broke through the lower layer of snow, and there they stayed with their loads, as though frozen to the earth, because of their weight and the congealed state of the old snow. Hannibal was compelled to give up the idea of attempting a detour, and, after clearing the snow away from the ridge, pitched camp there. Then he set his troops to work on the immensely laborious task of building up the path along the cliff. . . .

Battle of Cannae

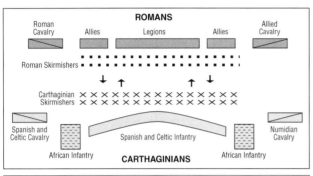

Stage 1. As the opposing armies prepare for battle, the Romans form ranks in their usual fashion, with their strongest infantry—made up of Roman legionaries—in the center, flanked by their allied infantry, and on the wings the Roman and allied cavalry units. Aware that the Romans mean to aim for his own center and overwhelm it, Hannibal moves his strongest infantry—the Africans—back to holding positions on the flanks and draws up his less formidable Spanish and Celtic infantry units in a crescent formation in the center. The battle opens with a clash of the light-armed skirmishers of the opposing sides.

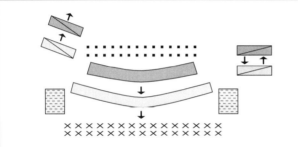

Stage 2. After the initial, indecisive exchange between the skirmishers, per the usual procedure they retreat to the rear and the opposing infantry units advance on each other. The Roman legions and allied units push the weaker Carthaginian center backward, just as Hannibal had anticipated they would, while he shrewdly continues to hold his Africans in reserve. Meanwhile, the cavalry units on the right clash, while on the left the Roman cavalry breaks and flees from the numerically superior Spanish and Celtic cavalry.

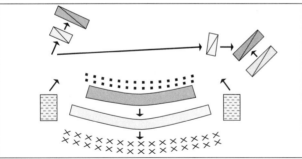

Stage 3. As the Roman infantrymen continue to press forward, believing they are winning the battle, Hannibal's brilliant trap begins to spring on them. With the added support of his skirmishers in the rear, his center holds. At the same time, his Africans turn toward the center and begin to envelop the Roman flanks. Meanwhile, as a small contingent of his Spanish and Celtic cavalry pursues the Roman horsemen off the field, the rest swing behind the Roman army and attack the Roman allied cavalry from the rear.

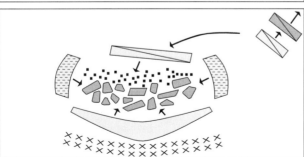

Stage 4. Assaulted front and back by the enemy, the Roman allied cavalry breaks and flees, pursued by Hannibal's Numidians. His Spanish and Celtic cavalry then wheels around and attacks the Roman center from behind. Now nearly surrounded, the normally disciplined Roman ranks fall apart and a massive slaughter ensues. Some 50,000 Romans are killed, the largest single battlefield loss in Rome's history, while Hannibal, whose victory is complete, loses only 6,000 to 7,000 men.

After he had reassembled all his forces Hannibal resumed the descent, and three days after leaving the precipice I have just described he arrived in the plains. He had lost many men at the hands of the enemy, at the various river crossings and in the course of his march, while the precipices and difficult passes of the Alps had cost not only many human lives but even greater numbers of horses and mules. The whole march from New Carthage had taken him five months, and the actual crossing of the Alps fifteen days.

Polybius, *The Histories,* published as *Polybius: The Rise of the Roman Empire,* trans. Ian Scott-Kilvert. New York: Penguin, 1979, pp. 227–28.

Catastrophe at Cannae

In 216 B.C., Hannibal delivered the Romans their worst defeat ever at Cannae, in southeastern Italy. As Livy recalls here, Hannibal cleverly used his Gallic and Spanish troops to lure the Romans into a trap, then unleashed his crack African troops on the enemy. As many as fifty thousand Romans lost their lives.

At dawn Hannibal first sent his light contingents, including the Baleares, across the river, then followed with his main force, drawing up in their battle positions the various contingents as they reached the other side. On his left, near the river bank, were the Gallic and Spanish horse, facing their Roman counterparts; on his right were the Numidians, and his centre was strongly held by infantry, so disposed as to have Gauls and Spaniards in the centre and African troops on each flank. To look at them, one might have thought the Africans were Roman soldiers—their arms were largely Roman, having been part of the spoils at Trasimene [where Hannibal had defeated the Romans], and some, too, at the Trebia. The Gallic and Spanish contingents carried shields of similar shape, but their swords were of different pattern, those of the Gauls being very long and not pointed, those of the Spaniards, who were accustomed to use them for piercing rather than cutting, being handily short and sharply pointed. One must admit, too, that the rest of the turn-out of these peoples, combined with their general appearance and great stature, made an awesome spectacle: the Gauls naked from the navel upwards; the Spaniards ranged in line in their dazzling white linen tunics bordered with purple. The total number of infantry in the battle-line was 40,000; of cavalry 10,000. The left wing was commanded by Hasdrubal, the right by Maharbal; Hannibal in person, supported by his brother Mago, held the centre. The Roman line faced south, the Carthaginian north; and luckily for both the early morning sun (whether they had taken up their positions by accident or design) shone obliquely on each of them; but a wind which had got up—called locally the Volturnus—was a disadvantage to the Romans as it carried clouds of dust into their eyes and obscured their vision.

The battle-cry rang out; the auxiliaries leapt forward, and with the light troops the action began. Soon the Gallic and Spanish horse on the Carthaginian left were engaged with the Roman right. Lack of space made it an unusual cavalry encounter:

the antagonists were compelled to charge head-on, front to front; there was no room for outflanking manoeuvres, as the river on one side and the massed infantry on the other pinned them in, leaving them no option but to go straight ahead. The horses soon found themselves brought to a halt, jammed close together in the inadequate space, and the riders set about dragging their opponents from the saddle, turning the contest more or less into an infantry battle. It was fierce while it lasted, but that was not for long; the Romans were forced to yield and hurriedly withdrew. Towards the end of this preliminary skirmish, the regular infantry became engaged; for a time it was an equal struggle, but at last the Romans, after repeated efforts, maintaining close formation on a broad front, drove in the opposing Gallic and Spanish troops, which were in wedge formation, projecting from the main body, and too thin to be strong enough to withstand the pressure. As these hurriedly withdrew, the Romans continued their forward thrust, carrying straight on through the broken column of the enemy now flying for their lives, until they reached the Carthaginian centre, after which, with little or no resistance, they penetrated to the position held by the African auxiliaries. These troops held the two Carthaginian wings, drawn back a little, while the centre, held by the Gauls and Spaniards, projected somewhat forward. The forcing back of the projecting wedge soon levelled the Carthaginian front; then, as under increasing pressure the beaten troops still further retired, the front assumed a concave shape, leaving the Africans on, as it were, the two projecting ends of the crescent. Recklessly the Romans charged straight into it, and the Africans on each side closed in. In another minute they had further extended their wings and closed the trap in the Roman rear.

The brief Roman success had been in vain. Now, leaving the Gauls and Spaniards on whom they had done much execution as they fled, they turned to face the Africans. This time the fight was by no means on equal terms: the Romans were surrounded, and—which was worse—they were tired men matched against a fresh and vigorous enemy.

Meanwhile the Roman left, where the allied horse confronted the Numidians, was also engaged. For a while things went slowly, owing to a Carthaginian ruse right at the outset. About 500 Numidians pretended to desert: in addition to their regular weapons they concealed swords under their tunics and rode up to the Roman line with their shields slung behind their backs. Suddenly dismounting, and flinging their shields and javelins on the ground, they were taken into the line by the Romans, and then conducted to the rear, where they were ordered to remain. While the general action was developing, they kept quiet enough; but as soon as no one in their vicinity had eyes or thoughts for anything but the progress of the battle, they picked up their shields from where they lay scattered around amongst the heaps of dead, and attacked the Roman line in the rear, striking at the soldiers' backs, hamstringing them, and causing terrible destruction, and even more panic and disorder.

It was at this juncture, when in one part of the field the Romans had little left but to try to save their skins, while in another, though hope was almost gone, they continued to fight with dogged determination, that Hasdrubal withdrew the Numidians from the centre, where they were not being used to much advantage, and sent them in pursuit of the scattered fugitives, at the same time ordering the Spaniards and Gauls to move to the support of the Africans, who by now were almost exhausted by what might be called butchery rather than battle.

Paullus [one of the Roman consuls], on the other wing, had been severely wounded by a sling-stone right at the start of the fight; none the less, at the head of his men in close order, he continued to make a number of attempts to get at Hannibal, and in several places succeeded in pulling things together. He had with him a guard of Roman cavalry, but the time came when Paullus was too weak even to control his horse, and they were obliged to dismount. Someone, it is said, told Hannibal that the consul had ordered his cavalry to dismount, and Hannibal, knowing they were therefore done for, replied that he might as well have delivered them up to him in chains.

The enemy's victory was now assured, and the dismounted cavalry fought in the full knowledge of defeat; they made no attempt to escape, preferring to die where they stood; and their refusal to budge, by delaying total victory even for a moment, further incensed the triumphant enemy, who unable to drive them from their ground, mercilessly cut them down. Some few survivors did indeed turn and run, wounded and worn out though they were.

Livy, *The History of Rome from Its Foundation*, Books 21–30 published as *Livy: The War with Hannibal*, trans. Aubrey de Sélincourt. New York: Penguin, 1972, pp. 145–48.

Rome Imposes Peace Terms on Carthage

Incredibly, the resilient Romans rebounded from their loss at Cannae and won the Second Punic War. They then demanded certain peace terms, which Polybius records here. He also tells how Hannibal, who viewed these terms as lenient, convinced his countrymen to accept them.

The following were the heads of the terms proposed by the Romans. Carthage was to retain all the cities which she possessed in Africa before she commenced the late war against Rome, all her former territory together with flocks, herds, slaves and other property. From that day forward the Carthaginians should suffer no further injury, they should be governed by their own laws and customs, and would not have a Roman garrison quartered on them. These were the concessions made; the clauses of the opposite character were as follows.

The Carthaginians were to pay reparations to the Romans for all acts of injustice committed during the truce; prisoners of war and deserters who had fallen into their hands at any time were to be handed over; all their elephants and all ships of war with the exception of ten triremes were to be surrendered; they were not to make war on any people outside Africa at all, and on none in Africa without consent from Rome; they were to restore to Masinissa [king of Numidia, Carthage's

This engraving depicts Lucius Aemilius Paullus in a victory parade after having defeated the king of Macedonia, Perseus.

neighbor] all the houses, territory, cities and other property which had belonged to him or to his ancestors within the boundaries which would later be assigned to that king; they were to provide the Roman army with sufficient corn for three months and with pay until a reply should be received from Rome concerning the treaty; they were to pay an indemnity of 10,000 talents of silver over a period of fifty years in instalments of fifty Euboic talents each year; and they were to hand over as a guarantee of good faith 100 hostages. These were to be chosen by the Roman commander from among the young men of the country between the ages of fourteen and thirty. . . .

These were the terms which Scipio announced to the envoys, who as soon as the communication was complete hastened back to explain them to their fellow-countrymen in Carthage. On this occasion it is said that one of the senators decided to speak against the acceptance of the terms, and was actually beginning to do so when Hannibal came forward and forcibly pulled him down from the platform. When the other members showed their anger at such a breach of the traditions of the Senate, Hannibal rose to his feet and confessed that he had been at fault; if he acted in any way contrary to their customs, they must pardon him, since they knew that he had left Carthage when he was only nine, and had only now returned when he was past forty-five. He therefore appealed to them not to confine their attention to the question of whether he had violated the procedure of the house; they should rather consider whether or not he was genuinely concerned for his country, for this was the real reason why he had committed this misdemeanour. 'It seems to me amazing,' he told them, 'and indeed quite beyond my comprehension that anyone who is a citizen of Carthage and has full knowledge of the policies which we have both individually and collectively adopted against Rome should not thank his stars that now that we are at their mercy we have obtained such lenient terms. If you had been asked only a few days ago,' he continued, 'what you expected your country would suffer in the event of a Roman victory, the disasters which threatened us then appeared so overwhelming that you would not even have been able to express your fears. So now I beg you not even to debate the question, but to declare your acceptance of the proposals unanimously, to offer up sacrifices to the gods, and to pray with one voice that the Roman people may ratify the treaty.'

All the senators considered that this advice was as well-conceived as it was timely, and so they passed a resolution to conclude the treaty on the conditions set out above. The Senate then immediately sent out the envoys with instructions to accept the terms.

Polybius, *The Histories*, published as *Polybius: The Rise of the Roman Empire*, trans. Ian Scott-Kilvert. New York: Penguin, 1979, pp. 480–82.

Rome Plunders the Greek Lands

Soon after defeating Carthage a second time, the Romans turned eastward and attacked the Greeks. In this excerpt from his great history, Livy recounts how the Roman general Lucius Aemilius Paullus (or Paulus) ordered his soldiers to loot and wreck the towns of the Greek state of Epirus.

The consul himself made for Epirus and arrived at Passaron on the fifteenth day.

Not far from Passaron was the camp of Anicius. Paulus sent him a letter designed to prevent any disturbance about what was happening; he explained that the Senate had granted to his army the booty from those cities of Epirus that had gone over to Perseus [king of the Greek kingdom of Macedonia]. He then sent centurions to the different cities, who were to say that they had come to remove the garrisons so that the people of Epirus might be free, like the Macedonians. Ten leading members of each community were summoned by the consul, who directed them to have their gold and silver brought out to a public place. The consul then sent cohorts to all the cities, those bound for the more distant places setting out before those travelling to the nearer, so that they should all reach their destinations on the same day. The tribunes and centurions had been informed about what was afoot. Early in the morning all the gold and silver was collected; and at the fourth hour the troops were given the signal to plunder the towns. So great was the amount of booty that each cavalryman received 400 *denarii* in the distribution and each footsoldier 200, while 150,000 persons were taken away. The walls of the plundered cities—there were about seventy of them—were demolished. The entire booty was sold, and from the proceeds of the sale the sums mentioned above were paid out to the soldiers.

Livy, *The History of Rome from Its Foundation*, Books 31–45 published as *Livy: Rome and the Mediterranean*, trans. Henry Bettenson. New York: Penguin, 1976, pp. 633–34.

The Sack of Corinth

The culmination of Rome's conquest of the Greek lands was its brutal destruction of the once beautiful city of Corinth in 146 B.C. No detailed accounts of the sack have survived, but the second-century A.D. Greek traveler Pausanias left behind this short summary.

Mummius held back for the time being from entering Corinth even though the gates were open, suspecting there might be an ambush inside the walls, but two days after the battle he took possession in force and burnt Corinth. Most of the people who were left there were murdered by the Romans, and Mummius auctioned the women and children. He auctioned the slaves as well, those of them I mean who were set free and fought beside the Achaians [Greeks who had courageously stood up to the invading Romans] and were not killed at once in the fighting. He collected the most marvellous of sacred dedications and works of art, and gave the less important things to Attalos's general Philopoimen: and in my time at Pergamon [in Asia Minor] they still had the spoils of Corinth. Mummius broke down the walls and confiscated the armaments of every city that had fought against the Romans even before Rome sent out its advisory commission, and when his commissioners arrived he put an end to the democracies and established government by property qualification. Greece was taxed and the monied classes were barred from the acquisition of property abroad. All national leagues alike were put an end to, Achaian and Phokian or Boiotian or anywhere.

Pausanias, *Guide to Greece,* trans. Peter Levi. 2 vols. New York: Penguin, 1971, vol. 1, p. 267.

Chapter

2

Julius Caesar's Exploits and Conquests

Julius Caesar is the most famous of all ancient Roman figures and, with the exception of Jesus of Nazareth, arguably the best-known person produced by the ancient Western world. Indeed, states one of Caesar's many modern biographers, "Hardly any other figure has left such an enduring impression on posterity."[1] That impression derives from the long list of Caesar's exploits and achievements. He was one of the greatest military generals of all time, proving his leadership abilities in campaign after campaign. His conquest of Gaul (now France and Belgium) added large new territories to the Roman realm, lands that eventually became a key food-producing area. He also wrote a journal of this and other conquests (his *War Commentaries*), which survived the ages to become required reading in many European schools. In addition, he won an immense civil war and made himself dictator of Rome, soon after which he met his doom in probably the most renowned assassination plot in history. Finally, his blueprint for an autocratic Roman government was borrowed and modified by his adopted son, Octavian, who became Augustus, the first Roman emperor.

These are the major and familiar facts of Caesar's illustrious life, as seen from afar by generation after generation. They suggest that he must have been a larger-than-life individual, for no ordinary person could have accomplished so much; however, the fact that Caesar was hugely successful and influential does not alone convey what sort of man he was. His specific talents and character traits emerge from assorted surviving remarks by his contemporaries and other ancients closer to him in time. These snippets reveal an extraordinarily complex man who could be ambitious, ruthless, and brutal on the one hand and affable, generous, and constructive on the other.

Caesar's ruthless side was revealed partly in the large numbers of casualties he inflicted on his enemies. The first-century scholar Pliny the Elder wrote: "I would not credit to his glory the fact that . . . he killed 1,192,000 men in battle—a very great wrong against the human race. . . . He himself admitted as much by not publishing the details of the slaughter resulting from the civil wars."[2] Ancient accounts also tell how, in his term as consul (in 59 B.C.), Caesar ran the government like a gangster, freely employing illegal tactics.

In contrast, Caesar's positive gifts were abundant. The great orator and politician Cicero, who knew Caesar well and usually opposed him, could not deny his enemy's keen intelligence, literary skills, courage, daring, and resolve. Pliny also emphasized Caesar's intellect, recalling "his intrinsic vigor and quickness of mind, winged, as it

This bust shows Julius Caesar in the mid-40s B.C., shortly before his assassination in the Roman Senate.

were, with fire."[3] It was this unusual mix of admirable and disreputable traits that made Caesar successful, helped propel him to the heights of power, filled his enemies with envy and fear, and made him memorable to all future generations.

Notes

1. Christian Meier, *Caesar,* trans. David McLintock. New York: HarperCollins, 1996, p. 15.
2. Pliny the Elder, *Natural History,* excerpted in *Pliny the Elder: Natural History: A Selection,* trans. John H. Healy. New York: Penguin, 1991, p. 89.
3. Pliny the Elder, *Natural History,* p. 89.

Caesar's Personal Attributes

The second-century A.D. Roman historian Suetonius wrote a biography of Caesar that contains the following information about the great general's appearance, talents, and leadership qualities.

Caesar is said to have been tall, fair, and well-built, with a rather broad face and keen, dark-brown eyes. His health was sound, apart from sudden comas and a tendency to nightmares which troubled him towards the end of his life; but he twice had epileptic fits while on campaign. He was something of a dandy, always keeping his head carefully trimmed and shaved; and has been accused of having certain other hairy parts of his body depilated with tweezers. His baldness was a disfigurement which his enemies harped upon, much to his exasperation; but he used to comb the thin strands of hair forward from his poll, and of all the honours voted him by the Senate and People, none pleased him so much as the privilege of wearing a laurel wreath on all occasions— he constantly took advantage of it.

His dress was, it seems, unusual: he had added wrist-length sleeves with fringes to his purple-striped senatorial tunic, and the belt which he wore over it was never tightly fastened—hence [Roman general and dictator] Sulla's warning to the aristocratic party: 'Beware of that boy with the loose clothes!' . . .

Caesar equalled, if he did not surpass, the greatest orators and generals the world had ever known. His prosecution of Dolabella [a former consul accused of corruption] unquestionably placed him in the first rank of advocates; and Cicero, discussing the matter in his *Brutus,* confessed that he knew no more eloquent speaker than Caesar 'whose style is chaste, pellucid, and grand, not to say noble'. Cicero also wrote to [the Roman historian] Cornelius Nepos:

> Very well, then! Do you know any man who, even if he has concentrated on the art of oratory to the exclusion of all else, can speak better than Caesar? Or anyone who makes so many witty remarks? Or whose vocabulary is so varied and yet so exact? . . .

Caesar was a most skilful swordsman and horseman, and showed surprising powers of endurance. He always led his army, more often on foot than in the saddle, went bareheaded in sun and rain alike, and could travel for long distances at incredible speed in a gig, taking very little luggage. If he reached an unfordable river he would either swim or propel himself across it on an inflated skin; and often arrived at his destination before the messengers whom he had sent ahead to announce his approach.

It is a disputable point which was the more remarkable when he went to war: his caution or his daring. He never exposed his army to ambushes, but made careful reconnaissances; and refrained from crossing over into Britain until he had collected reliable information about

This statue of Julius Caesar portrays him as an imposing individual.

his way through the enemy outposts to take command on the spot. . . .

Though turning a blind eye to much of their misbehaviour, and never laying down any fixed scale of penalties, he allowed no deserter or mutineer to escape severe punishment. Sometimes, if a victory had been complete enough, he relieved the troops of all military duties and let them carry on as wildly as they pleased. One of his boasts was: 'My soldiers fight just as well when they are stinking of perfume.' He always addressed them not as 'My soldiers', but as 'Comrades . . . ', which put them into a better humour; and he equipped them splendidly. The silver and gold inlay of their weapons both improved their appearance on parade and made them more careful not to get disarmed in battle, these being objects of great value. Caesar loved his men dearly; when news came that Titurius' command had been massacred, he swore neither to cut his hair nor to trim his beard until they had been avenged.

By these means he won the devotion of his army as well as making it extraordinarily brave. At the outbreak of the Civil War every centurion in every legion volunteered to equip a cavalryman from his savings; and the private soldiers unanimously offered to serve under him without pay or rations, pooling their money so that nobody should go short. Throughout the entire struggle not a single Caesarian deserted.

Suetonius, *Lives of the Twelve Caesars,* published as *The Twelve Caesars,* trans. Robert Graves, rev. Michael Grant. New York: Penguin, 1979, pp. 34, 38, 40, 42–43.

the harbours there, the best course to steer, and the navigational risks. On the other hand, when news reached him that his camp in Germany was being besieged, he disguised himself as a Gaul and picked

Caesar Versus the Pirates

When Caesar was still a young man, he demonstrated his courage, boldness, and military talent when he dealt with pirates who had captured him in hopes of collecting a ransom. This account of the incident was recorded by Plutarch in his biography of Caesar.

First, when the pirates demanded a ransom of twenty talents, Caesar burst out laughing. They did not know, he said, who it was that they had captured, and he volunteered to pay fifty. Then, when he had sent his followers to the various cities in order to raise the money and was left with one friend and two servants among these Cilicians, about the most bloodthirsty people in the world, he treated them so highhandedly that, whenever he wanted to sleep, he would send to them and tell them to stop talking. For thirty-eight days, with the greatest unconcern, he joined in all their games and exercises, just as if he was their leader instead of their prisoner. He also wrote poems and speeches which he read aloud to them, and if they failed to admire his work, he would call them to their faces illiterate savages, and would often laughingly threaten to have them all hanged. They were much taken with this and attributed his freedom of speech to a kind of simplicity in his character or boyish playfulness. However, the ransom arrived from Miletus and, as soon as he had paid it and been set free, he immediately manned some ships and set sail from the harbour of Miletus against the pirates. He found them still there, lying at anchor off the island, and he captured nearly all of them. He took their property as spoils of war and put the men themselves into the prison at Pergamum. He then went in person to Junius, the governor of Asia, thinking it proper that he, as praetor in charge of the province, should see to the punishment of the prisoners. Junius, however, cast longing eyes at the money, which came to a considerable sum, and kept saying that he needed time to look into the case. Caesar paid no further attention to him. He went to Pergamum, took the pirates out of prison and crucified the lot of them, just as he had often told them he would do when he was on the island and they imagined that he was joking.

Plutarch, *Life of Caesar*, in *Fall of the Roman Republic: Six Lives by Plutarch*, trans. Rex Warner. New York: Penguin, 1972, p. 245.

Caesar Invades Britain

In 55 B.C., in the midst of his conquest of Gaul (what is now France), Caesar sailed eighty troop transports across the English Channel and created a beachhead in southern Britain. This account of the landing is his own, from his famous War Commentaries.

We could see the enemy's armed forces lined up all along the cliffs. At this point there was a narrow beach with high hills behind it, so that it was possible to hurl weapons down from the higher ground onto the shore. It seemed to me an extremely bad place to effect a landing, and so we waited at anchor until about three thirty P.M. for the rest of the ships to join us. During this time I summoned the generals and high-ranking officers . . . and told them what I wanted done. I warned them that the tactical demands of warfare in general—and especially so on sea, where things can happen quickly and unpredictably—require that orders must be carried out instantly and on the spot. The meeting was then dismissed. We had both the wind and the tide in our favor; the signal was given to weigh anchor and, after moving on about eight miles, we ran the ships ashore on an open, evenly shelved beach.

The natives, however, had realized what we planned to do. They had sent their cavalry and their chariots (a type of weapon which they nearly always use in battle) on ahead. The rest of their troops followed behind, and they now stood ready to oppose our landing. Things were very difficult for us indeed, and for the following reasons. Our ships were too big to be run ashore except where the water was deep; the troops knew nothing of the ground on which they were to fight and not only had their hands full but were weighed down by the heavy armor which they carried; they had to jump down from

Caesar (standing left) directs his troops in his first invasion of Britain in 55 B.C. The expedition was unsuccessful, partly because a series of storms badly damaged his ships.

the transports, get a footing in the surf, and fight the enemy all at the same time. The enemy, on the other hand, were quite unencumbered and knew the ground well. Either standing on dry land or going a little way into the water, they hurled their weapons boldly at us and spurred on their horses, which were trained for this sort of fighting. All this had a most disturbing effect on our men. They had no experience at all of this sort of warfare, and they failed to show the fire and enthusiasm which could always be expected of them in battles on land.

When I saw what the situation was I ordered the warships—which were swifter and easier to handle than the transports and at the same time were of a shape which the natives had scarcely ever seen before—to move clear of the transports, to row forward at full speed and then run ashore on the enemy's exposed flank; from this position they were to make use of slings, arrows, and artillery to drive the enemy back and clear the beach. This maneuver proved to be extremely useful to us. The natives were greatly disturbed by the shape of the ships, the moving of the oars, and the strange machines used as artillery. They came to a halt and then fell back, though only a little way. Then, as our men still hesitated, chiefly because of the depth of the water, the man who carried the eagle of the Tenth Legion, after praying to the gods that what he was going to do would bring good luck to the legion, shouted out in a loud voice: "Come on, men! Jump, unless you want

to lose your eagle to the enemy. I, in any case, will do my duty to my country and to my general." He then threw himself from the ship and began to go toward the enemy, carrying the eagle with him. He was followed by all the rest, who jumped into the sea together, shouting out to each other that they must not disgrace themselves by losing their eagle. When the men from the next ships saw them, they followed their example and also began to move toward the enemy.

Julius Caesar, *Commentary on the Gallic War,* in *War Commentaries of Caesar,* trans. Rex Warner. New York: New American Library, 1960, pp. 81–82.

The Battle for Alesia

Perhaps the largest single battle of Caesar's Gallic campaigns occurred in 52 B.C. He laid siege to Alesia, stronghold of the great war chief Vercingetorix, and, as Caesar himself tells it, he soon found himself facing a huge army of reinforcements from all quarters.

After sending out scouts to reconnoiter this position, the enemy commanders chose out of their whole force sixty thousand men from the states [Gallic tribes] that had the greatest military reputation, secretly decided upon their objectives and their plan of action, and fixed the hour of noon as the moment for launching the attack.

This force was to be led by the Arvernian Vercassivellaunus, one of their four supreme commanders, and a relative of Vercingetorix. He left camp soon after

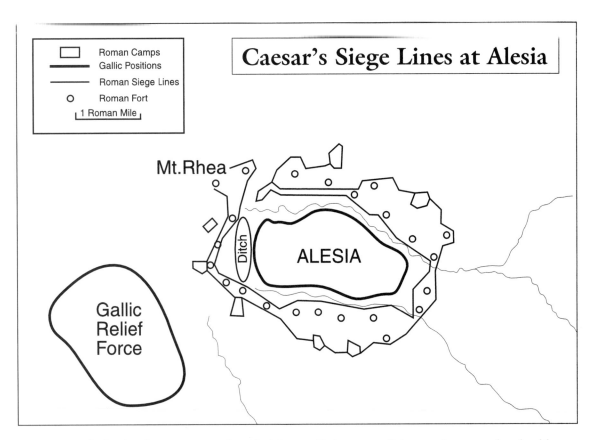

Caesar's Siege Lines at Alesia

Roman Camps
Gallic Positions

Roman Siege Lines

O   Roman Fort

1 Roman Mile

Mt.Rhea

Ditch

ALESIA

Gallic Relief Force

sunset and had almost completed his march before the sun rose. He concealed his troops in the shelter of the hill and told them to rest there after their night's work. When he saw that it was almost midday, he began to move toward that camp of ours which I have already described. At the same moment the Gallic cavalry advanced toward our entrenchments in the plain and the rest of their army appeared drawn up for action in front of their camp.

From the citadel of Alesia, Vercingetorix could see his countrymen going into action. He now led his own forces out of the town, bringing with him the hurdles, poles, mantlets, grappling hooks, and all the rest of the equipment that had been prepared for the sortie. Simultaneous attacks were made all along our lines and every sort of method was used by the Gauls, who were quick to concentrate at any point where the defense seemed likely to crack. Our men, strung out over such a huge area of fortification, did not find it easy to meet these attacks coming from so many different quarters. Another thing which had a most disturbing effect on them was the noise of shouting which they could hear behind them as they were fighting. This made them realize that their own safety depended on the courage that others might, or might not, show. It is,

This drawing shows how Caesar set up his siege works at Alesia, including guard towers, an earthen mound topped by a wooden palisade, a deep moat, and numerous booby traps.

indeed, generally the case that people are much more frightened of what they cannot see than of what they can.

I found a good place from which to see what was happening all along the line, and sent up reinforcements to sectors where our men were in difficulties. Both sides realized that this was the critical moment, the moment that called for a supreme effort. The Gauls knew that for them everything was lost unless they could break through our lines. The Romans saw in front of them, if they could only stand firm, the end of all their labors. Our difficulties were greatest at the fortifications on the hill where, as already mentioned, Vercassivellaunus had been sent. Here the unfavorable downward slope was a factor which told heavily against us. Some of the enemy hurled javelins down on us, while others advanced with locked shields in

"tortoise" formation, and all the time fresh troops were ready to replace those who were exhausted. The whole Gallic force heaped earth up against the fortifications, thus making it possible for them to climb the rampart, at the same time covering over all the traps which we had hidden in the ground. Our men's supply of weapons was running short and their strength too was beginning to fail them.

Seeing what the position was and how distressed they were, I sent Labienus with six cohorts to their relief. I told him that if he found it impossible to hold the position, he must regroup the cohorts and fight his way out; but he must not do this unless it was absolutely necessary. I myself went to visit other sectors of the line, urging the men to fight on and not give in, and telling them that everything they had won in former battles was now at stake and depended on this day and on this hour.

The Gauls attacking our inner lines gave up hope of being able to break through in the direction of the plain; our defense works were on too big a scale. They now attempted to storm through our lines on the higher and more broken ground and brought up all their equipment to these points. The defenders were driven from the towers by a hail of weapons. The enemy then proceeded to fill up the trenches with hurdles and earth and to tear down the rampart and breastwork with their grappling hooks. First I sent young Brutus to the threatened spot with some cohorts, then the general Gaius Fabius with some more; and finally, as the fighting grew fiercer still, I led up fresh troops myself to the relief. When the position was restored and the enemy driven back, I hurried to the sector where I had sent Labienus. I withdrew four cohorts from the nearest redoubt and ordered some of the cavalry to follow me while other detachments were instructed to ride around the outer lines and attack the enemy in the rear.

Meanwhile Labienus had found that neither rampart nor trench had been able to hold up the furious attacks of the enemy. Fortunately he had been able to collect together eleven cohorts from the nearest redoubts. He now sent messengers to me to tell me what he thought should be done. I hurried on so as to be able to take part in the action.

The enemy could see that I was coming because of the scarlet cloak which I always wore to mark me out in action. And as the lower slopes along which I came were visible from the higher ground, they could also see the squadrons of cavalry and the cohorts which I had ordered to follow me. So the enemy rushed into battle. The shout was raised on both sides and was taken up by an answering shout from the men on the ramparts and along the whole line of entrenchments. Our men dispensed with javelins and got to work with their swords. Suddenly the Gauls saw our cavalry coming in from the rear; fresh cohorts of infantry were also bearing down. The enemy turned and ran. As they ran, the cavalry were upon them. There was a great slaughter. Sedulius, the commander and chief of the Lemovices, was killed; Vercassivellaunus, the Arvernian, was taken prisoner in the rout; seventy-four Gallic war standards were brought in to me. Out of all that great army very few got safely back to camp.

From the town the Gauls saw the rout and slaughter of their countrymen and, abandoning all hope of relief, withdrew their troops from our fortifications. There was an immediate flight too from the Gallic camp as soon as the news of the battle was received. Indeed if our soldiers had not been exhausted by the hard work they had done all through the day and the constant calls that had been made on them to reinforce threatened points, the entire enemy army could have been destroyed. As it was, our cavalry, which I sent out about midnight, caught up with their rear guard and killed and captured great numbers of them. The rest fled to the various states from which they had come.

Julius Caesar, *Commentary on the Gallic War*, in *War Commentaries of Caesar*, trans. Rex Warner. New York: New American Library, 1960, pp. 179–80.

Caesar Crosses the Rubicon

On January 10, 49 B.C., Caesar defied the Senate, which had ordered him to lay down command of his army, and crossed the Rubicon River, igniting a civil war. As many ancient accounts do, this one by Suetonius incorporates supernatural elements to dramatize a pivotal event.

Caesar overtook his advanced guard at the river Rubicon, which formed the frontier between Gaul and Italy. Well aware how critical a decision confronted him, he turned to his staff, remarking: 'We may still draw back but, once across that little bridge, we shall have to fight it out.'

As he stood, in two minds, an apparition of superhuman size and beauty was seen sitting on the river bank playing a reed pipe. A party of shepherds gathered around to listen and, when some of Caesar's men, including some of the trumpeters, broke ranks to do the same, the apparition snatched a trumpet from one of them, ran down to the river, blew a thunderous blast, and crossed over. Caesar exclaimed: 'Let us accept this as a sign from the Gods, and follow where they beckon, in vengeance on our double-dealing enemies. The die is cast.'

Suetonius, *Lives of the Twelve Caesars*, published as *The Twelve Caesars*, trans. Robert Graves, rev. Michael Grant. New York: Penguin, 1979, pp. 27–28.

Alarm and Confusion in the Capital

As Caesar marched on Rome, his chief rival, Pompey, fled along with the two consuls and many senators. One of Rome's most distinguished senators, Cicero, penned this letter to a friend on January 22, 49 B.C., expressing his disappointment in Pompey's flight and deep apprehension about what the power-hungry Caesar might do.

It is civil war, though it has not sprung from division among our citizens but from the daring of one abandoned citizen. He is strong in military forces, he attracts adherents by hopes and promises, he covets the whole universe. Rome is delivered to him stripped of defenders, stocked with supplies: one may fear anything from one who regards her temples and her homes not as his native land but as his loot. What he will do, and how he will do it, in the absence of senate and magistrates, I do not know. He will be unable even to pretend constitutional methods. But where can our party raise its head, or when? You too remark how poor a general our leader [Pompey] is: why, he did not even know how things were in Picenum [Pompey's home territory, which Caesar captured]; and the crisis shows his lack of plan. Pass over other faults of the last ten years: what compromise were not better than this flight? I do not know what he is thinking of doing now, though I inquire by constant letters. It is agreed that his alarm and confusion have reached the limit. He was kept in Italy to garrison Rome, but no garrison or place to post a garrison can I see. We depend entirely upon two legions that were kept here by a trick and are practically disloyal. For so far the levy has found unwilling recruits, disinclined to fight. But the time of compromise is past. The future is obscure. We, or our leaders, have brought things to such a pass that, having put to sea without a rudder, we must trust to the mercy of the storm.

Quoted in Naphtali Lewis and Meyer Reinhold, eds., *Roman Civilization, Sourcebook I: The Republic.* New York: Harper and Row, 1966, pp. 283–84.

Caesar Defeats Pompey

In 48 B.C., Caesar crossed over to Greece and defeated Pompey at Pharsalus. In this excerpt from his Life of Caesar, *Plutarch describes the battle and the sad plight of Pompey, a great general who had never before lost a battle.*

As Caesar himself was just about to order his line to advance and was already going up towards the front, his eyes fell first on one of his centurions, a man who had proved reliable to him in the past and who had had experience of many campaigns. He was now urging on the men under his command and challenging them to compete with him in showing courage in action. Caesar called out to him by name and said: 'Well, Gaius

Crassinus, what are our prospects? How are we feeling about it?' Then Crassinus stretched out his right hand and shouted at the top of his voice: 'We shall win, Caesar, and win gloriously. And as for me, you shall praise me today, whether I am alive or dead at the end of it.' With these words he charged forwards at the double and, followed by 120 soldiers under his command, was the first man to engage the enemy. He hacked his way through the first rank and was still pressing forwards, cutting down men on all sides of him, when he was stopped by a blow of a sword which was thrust into his mouth with such force that it came out at the back of his neck.

So the two infantry armies joined battle and fought hand to hand. And now Pompey's cavalry rode up on the flank in a proud array and deployed their squadrons in order to encircle Caesar's right wing. Before they could charge, the cohorts which Caesar had posted behind him ran forward and, instead of hurling their javelins, as they usually did, or even thrusting at the thighs and legs of the enemy, aimed at their eyes and stabbed upwards at their faces. Caesar had instructed them to do this because he believed that these young men, who had not had much experience of battle and the wounds of battle but who particularly plumed themselves on their good looks, would dislike more than anything the idea of being attacked in this way and, fearing both the danger of the moment and the possibility of disfigurement for the future, would not be able to stand up to it. And in fact this was exactly what happened. They could not face the upward thrusts of the javelins or even the sight of the iron points; they turned their heads away and covered them up in their anxiety to keep their faces unscarred. Soon they were in complete disorder, and finally, in a most disgraceful way, they turned and fled, thereby ruining everything, since the cohorts who had defeated the cavalry at once swept round behind the infantry, fell on their rear, and began to cut them to pieces.

When Pompey, from the other wing, saw his cavalry routed and scattered, he was no longer the same person as before, and no longer remembered that he was Pompey the Great. Looking more like a man whom some god has deprived of his wits, he went off, without saying a word, to his tent and there sat down and waited for what was to come, until his whole army was routed and the enemy had begun to attack the fortifications of his camp and were fighting with the detachments who were guarding it. At this point he seemed to come to his senses. The only words he uttered were, so they say, 'What, into the camp too?' and, with these words, he took off his general's clothes and, changing into other clothes more suitable for a fugitive, stole away. I shall describe in my *Life of Pompey* what happened to him later, and how he put himself into the hands of the Egyptians and was murdered.

Plutarch, *Life of Caesar*, in *Fall of the Roman Republic: Six Lives by Plutarch*, trans. Rex Warner. New York: Penguin, 1972, pp. 287–88.

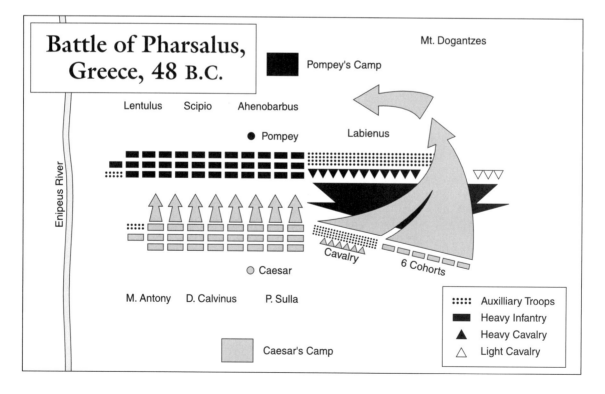

Caesar Meets Cleopatra

Caesar followed Pompey to Egypt, where the latter had been murdered by the local ruler, Ptolemy XIII. Plutarch here tells how Ptolemy's sister, Cleopatra, who opposed her brother, cleverly smuggled herself into Caesar's chamber in the palace.

Cleopatra, taking only one of her friends with her (Apollodorus the Sicilian), embarked in a small boat and landed at the palace when it was already getting dark. Since there seemed to be no other way of getting in unobserved, she stretched herself out at full length inside a sleeping bag, and Apollodorus, after tying up the bag, carried it indoors to Caesar. This little trick of Cleopatra's, which showed her provocative impudence, is said to have been the first thing about her which captivated Caesar, and, as he grew to know her better, he was overcome by her charm and arranged that she and her brother should be reconciled and should share the throne of Egypt together.

Plutarch, *Life of Caesar*, in *Fall of the Roman Republic: Six Lives by Plutarch*, trans. Rex Warner. New York: Penguin Books, 1972, p. 290.

Caesar's Dictatorship

Having won the great civil war, Caesar returned to Rome and declared himself dictator for life. As explained in this passage by Suetonius, Caesar immediately embarked on a series of reforms of various kinds, including creating a new calendar, and began to hatch even more grandiose plans that never came to fruition.

Caesar next turned his attention to domestic reforms. First he reorganized the Calendar which the College of Priests had allowed to fall into such disorder, by inserting days or months as it suited them, that the harvest and vintage festivals no longer corresponded with the appropriate seasons. He linked the year to the course of the sun by lengthening it [from 355 days] to 365 days, abolishing the short extra month and adding an entire day every fourth year. But to make the next first of January fall at the right season, he drew out this particular year [46 B.C.] by two extra months, inserted between November and December, so that it consisted of fifteen, including the intercalary one inserted after February in the old style.

He brought the Senate up to strength by creating new patricians, and increased the yearly quota of praetors, aediles, and quaestors, as well as of minor officials; reinstating those degraded by the Censors or condemned for corruption by a jury. Also, he arranged with the commons that, apart from the Consul, half the magistrates should be popularly elected and half nominated by himself. Allowing even the sons of proscribed men to stand, he circulated brief directions to the voters. For instance: 'Caesar the Dictator to such-and-such a tribe of voters: I recommend So-and-so to you for office.' He limited jury service to knights and senators, disqualifying the Treasury tribunes.

Caesar changed the old method of registering voters: he made the city landlords help him to complete the list, street by street, and reduced from 320,000 to 150,000 the number of householders who might draw free grain. To do away with the nuisance of having to summon everyone for enrolment periodically, he made the practors keep their register up to date by replacing the names of dead men with those of others not yet listed.

Since the population of Rome had been considerably diminished by the transfer of 80,000 men to overseas colonies, he forbade any citizen between the ages of twenty and forty, who was not serving in the army, to absent himself from Italy for more than three years in succession. Nor might any senator's son travel abroad unless as a member of some magistrate's household or staff; and at least a third of the cattlemen employed by graziers had to be free-born. Caesar also granted the citizenship to all medical practitioners and professors of liberal arts resident in Rome, thus inducing them to remain and tempting others to follow suit.

He disappointed popular agitators by cancelling no debts, but in the end decreed that every debtor should have his property assessed according to pre-war valuation and, after deducting the interest already paid directly, or by way of a banker's guarantee, should satisfy his creditors with whatever sum that might represent. This left debtors with perhaps a fourth part of their property. Caesar dissolved all workers' guilds except the ancient ones, and increased the penalties for crime; and since wealthy men had less compunction about committing major offences, because the worst that could happen to them was a sentence of exile, he punished murderers of fellow-citizens (as Cicero records) by the seizure of either their entire property, or half of it.

In his administration of justice he was both conscientious and severe, and went so far as to degrade senators found guilty of extortion. Once, when an ex-praetor married a woman on the day after her divorce from another man, he annulled the union, although adultery between them was not suspected.

He imposed a tariff on foreign manufactures; forbade the use, except on stated occasions, of litters and the wearing of either scarlet robes or pearls by those below a certain rank and age. To implement his laws against luxury he placed inspectors in different parts of the market to seize delicacies offered for sale in violation of his orders; sometimes he even sent lictors and guards into dining-rooms to remove illegal dishes, already served, which his watchmen had failed to intercept.

Caesar continually undertook great new works for the embellishment of the city, or for the Empire's protection and enlargement. His first projects were a temple of Mars, the biggest in the world, to build which he would have had to fill up and pave the lake where the naval sham-fight had been staged; and an enormous theatre sloping down from the Tarpeian Rock on the Capitoline Hill.

Another task he set himself was the reduction of the Civil Code to manageable proportions, by selecting from the unwieldy mass of statutes only the most essential, and publishing them in a few volumes. Still another was to provide the finest possible public libraries, by commissioning Marcus Varro to collect and classify Greek and Latin books. His engineering schemes included the draining of the Pomptine Marshes and of Lake Fucinus; also a highway running from the Adriatic across the Apennines to the Tiber; and a canal to be cut through the Isthmus of Corinth. In the military field he planned an expulsion of the Dacians from the Black Sea area and Thrace, which they had recently occupied, and then an attack on Parthia [Persia] by way of Lesser Armenia; but decided not to risk a pitched battle until he had familiarized himself with Parthian tactics.

All these schemes were cancelled by his assassination.

Suetonius, *Lives of the Twelve Caesars,* published as *The Twelve Caesars,* trans. Robert Graves, rev. Michael Grant. New York: Penguin, 1979, pp. 31–33.

Death in the Senate

In 44 B.C., a number of Roman senators opposed to Caesar's dictatorship conspired to kill him. Of the several ancient accounts of the deed that have survived, this one, from Plutarch's biography of Brutus, is rarely quoted from today. One of the ringleaders of the conspiracy, Brutus may have been Caesar's illegitimate son.

For now news was brought that Caesar was coming, carried in a litter. For, being discouraged by the ill-omens that attended his sacrifice, he had determined to undertake no affairs of any great importance that day, but to defer them till another time, excusing himself that he was sick. As soon as he came out of his litter, Popilius Laenas, he who but a little before had wished Brutus good success in his undertaking, coming up to him, conversed a great while with him, Caesar standing still all the while, and seeming to be very attentive. The conspirators (to give them this name), not being able to hear what he said, but guessing by what themselves were conscious of that this conference was the discovery of their treason, were again disheartened, and, looking upon one another, agreed from each other's countenances that they should not stay to be taken, but should all kill themselves. And now when Cassius and some others were laying hands upon their daggers under their robes, and were drawing them out, Brutus, viewing narrowly the looks and gesture of Laenas, and finding that he was earnestly petitioning and not accusing, said nothing, because there were many strangers to the conspiracy mingled amongst them, but by a cheerful countenance encouraged Cassius. And after a little while, Laenas, having kissed Caesar's hand, went away, showing plainly that all his discourse was about some particular business relating to himself.

Now when the senate was gone in before to the chamber where they were to sit, the rest of the company placed themselves close about Caesar's chair, as if they had some suit to make to him, and Cassius, turning his face to Pompey's statue, is said to have invoked it, as if it had been sensible of his prayers. Trebonius, in

Caesar lies murdered at the base of Pompey's statue. In the background the conspirators celebrate the end of his dictatorship.

the meanwhile, engaged Antony's attention at the door, and kept him in talk outside. When Caesar entered, the whole senate rose up to him. As soon as he was sat down, the men all crowded round about him, and set Tillius Cimber, one of their own number, to intercede in behalf of his brother that was banished; they all joined their prayers with his, and took Caesar by the hand, and kissed his head and his breast. But he putting aside at first their supplications, and afterwards, when he saw they would not desist, violently rising up, Tillius with both hands caught hold of his robe and pulled it off from his shoulders, and Casca, that stood behind him, drawing his dagger, gave him the first, but a slight wound, about the shoulder. Caesar snatching hold of the handle of the dag-

ger, and crying out aloud in Latin, "Villain Casca, what do you?" he, calling in Greek to his brother, bade him come and help. And by this time, finding himself struck by a great many hands, and looking around about him to see if he could force his way out, when he saw Brutus with his dagger drawn against him, he let go Casca's hand, that he had hold of, and covering his head with his robe, gave up his body to their blows. And they so eagerly pressed towards the body, and so many daggers were hacking together, that they cut one another; Brutus, particularly, received a wound in his hand, and all of them were besmeared with the blood.

Plutarch, *Life of Brutus,* in *Lives of the Noble Grecians and Romans,* trans. John Dryden. New York: Random House, 1932, pp. 1195–96.

The Reign of Augustus, the First Emperor

The reign of Augustus Caesar (30 B.C.–A.D. 14) marked a crucial transition in the Roman world. As Octavian, the calculating and shrewd adopted son of Julius Caesar, he had forced his way into the corridors of Roman power and defeated all his rivals in the last of the destructive civil wars of the first century B.C. When the dust had settled, the Roman Republic was in ruins and the Roman people were war weary, bitter, and fearful of the future. With the sharp intuitiveness of a great politician, Octavian seemed to sense that everyone—rich and poor, former friends and former enemies—was ready for a leader who promised to heal the nation. Seizing the opportunity, almost overnight he transformed himself from an ambitious

power broker into Augustus, "the revered one," a benign dictator and beneficent father figure dedicated to restoring order to Rome and safety and confidence to its people.

Augustus succeeded in this incredibly ambitious venture, in part because, as an absolute ruler, his plans and policies met no significant opposition. Though he kept the Senate and most other republican symbols in place, in every matter he had the last word. Also, his policies were largely constructive, so few if any had any desire to oppose them. Most importantly, Augustus ruled a long time—more than four decades—in which he shepherded the realm farther and farther away from the chaos and unhappiness of the past and closer and closer toward a promised future of prosperity and content. As the second-century historian Dio Cassius pointed out:

> The great majority of those who had lived under the Republic were now dead. . . . The later generation knew nothing of that form of government. They had been brought up entirely or very largely under the conditions which prevailed during the Principate [the new imperial system], and so not only did they find no objection to them . . . but even rejoiced in them, since they saw that their present situation was preferable and more free from fear than those times of which they knew from hearsay.[1]

Thus, Augustus's reign bridged the gap between the Republic and the Empire. His rule was characterized by peace, honest and caring government, large-scale urban renewal, the revival of traditional Roman morals (seen to have been lost in the civil war era), and generous patronage of literature and the arts. Stressing such themes, Augustus led the Roman world into what later came to be called the Pax Romana, or "Roman Peace," which lasted nearly two centuries. Few of his immediate successors to the throne were as enlightened as he was, yet most were competent enough that Rome reached its height of size, prosperity, and magnificence about a century after his passing.

A drawing of the famous statue of Augustus found in his wife's villa at Prima Porta.

Notes

1. Dio Cassius, *Roman History: The Reign of Augustus*, trans. Ian Scott-Kilvert. New York: Penguin, 1987, pp. 256–57.

The Second Triumvirate

Octavian, the future Augustus, shrewdly gained power by convincing his rivals, the generals Antony and Lepidus, to form the Second Triumvirate in 43 B.C. In this excerpt from his history of Rome, the second-century A.D. Romanized Greek historian Appian describes the triumvirs' fateful first meeting, in which they carved up the Roman world and compiled lists of their enemies.

Octavian and Antonius [Antony] met near Mutina, on a small low-lying island in the river Lavinius, to exchange enmity for friendship. Each had five legions, which they left drawn up facing each other while they each advanced with 300 men to the bridges over the river. Lepidus went ahead in person to search the island, and signalled with his cloak to each of them to come across. They then left their 300 men with their advisers at the bridges and went forward in full view into the space between, where the three of them sat down together, with Octavian in the centre presiding because of his office. They met for two days, from dawn until dusk, and their decisions were as follows: Octavian would resign the consulship to Ventidius for the remainder of the year, and a new office charged with the resolution of the civil wars would be created by law for Lepidus, Antonius, and Octavian. They would hold this office for five years, and it would have an authority equal to that of the consuls. This was the title they decided to use, instead of dictators. . . .

They were to appoint immediately the annual magistrates at Rome for five years ahead, and they distributed the provincial governorships in such a way that Antonius received the whole of Gaul except for the part adjoining the Pyrenees, which they call Old Gaul; this was to be held by Lepidus, along with Spain; and Octavian was to have Africa, Sardinia, Sicily, and any other islands in that area. Thus the three distributed the Roman Empire among themselves. The only territories whose allocation they postponed were those to the east of the Adriatic, because these were still controlled by Brutus and Cassius [leaders of the conspiracy to kill Caesar] against whom Antonius and Octavian were to campaign. Lepidus was to become consul in the following year and stay in Rome because he would be needed there. He would govern Spain through deputies, while three legions from his army would be kept by himself to meet his needs in Rome and seven would be divided between Octavian and Antonius—three to Octavian and four to Antonius, so that each of them could take twenty legions to the war. . . .

In this way they divided up the best parts of Italy among their soldiers. They also decided to put their private enemies to death early on, to prevent them causing trouble to themselves as they put these arrangements into effect while simultaneously conducting a war outside Italy. Such were their decisions, which they recorded in writing. . . .

The triumvirs withdrew privately to put together a list of those who were to die. They marked down not only the powerful men they mistrusted, but also their own private foes. In exchange, they surrendered their own relations and friends to each other, both then and later. Extra names were constantly added to the list, some from enmity, others only because they had been a nuisance, or were friends of enemies, or enemies of friends, or were notably wealthy. They needed, you understand, a great deal of money for the war. Brutus and Cassius were profiting from the taxes of Asia, both those which had already been paid and those that were still coming in, and from the support of kings and satraps, while they themselves, whose base was Europe and particularly Italy, which had been worn out by wars and financial exactions, were short of resources. For this reason the triumvirs finally imposed savage demands for money even on ordinary male citizens and women, and invented duties on sales and leases. The point was reached where a person was proscribed [condemned] because he had a fine house in town or country. The total of those condemned to death and confiscation of property was about 300 senators and 2,000 equestrians. These included brothers and uncles

Octavian, Antony, and Lepidus hold the first meeting of the Second Triumvirate. They divided up the Roman world among themselves and compiled a list of political enemies.

of the men who proscribed them and of their subordinates, if they had done anything to offend the leaders or these subordinates.

Appian, *Roman History,* excerpted in *Appian: The Civil Wars,* trans. John Carter. New York: Penguin, 1996, pp. 209–11.

The Roman World's Fate Is Decided at Actium

In time the Second Triumvirate shattered and Octavian squared off with Antony for control of the Roman world. In 31 B.C., with the help of his associate Marcus Agrippa, Octavian defeated Antony and Antony's ally, Cleopatra, at Actium, in western Greece. The second-century A.D. Roman historian Dio Cassius recorded this vivid account of the battle.

So the fleets came to grips and the battle began. Each side uttered loud shouts to the men aboard, urging the troops to summon up their prowess and their fighting spirit, and the men could also hear a babel of orders being shouted at them from those on shore.

The two sides used different tactics. Octavian's fleet, having smaller and faster ships, could advance at speed and ram the enemy, since their armour gave them protection on all sides. If they sank a vessel, they had achieved their object; if not, they would back water before they could be engaged at close quarters, and either ram the same ship suddenly a second time, or let it go and turn against others. When they had damaged these as much as they could in a short time, they would seek out fresh opponents over and over again, constantly switching their attack, so that their onslaught always came where it was least expected. They feared their adversaries' long-range missiles no less than their superior strength in fighting at close quarters, and so they wasted no time either in the approach or the clash. They would sail up suddenly so as to close with their target before the enemy's archers could hit them, inflict damage or cause enough confusion to escape being grappled, and then quickly back away out of range.

Antony's tactics, on the other hand, were to pour heavy volleys of stones and arrows upon the enemy ships as they approached, and then try to entrap them with iron grapnels. When they could reach their targets, Antony's ships got the upper hand, but if they missed, their own hulls would be pierced by the rams and they would sink, or else, in the attempt to avoid collision, they would lose time and expose themselves to attack by other ships. Two or three of Octavian's vessels would fall upon one of Antony's, with some inflicting all the damage they could, while the others bore the brunt of the counter-attack.

On the one side the helmsmen and rowers suffered the heaviest casualties, on the other the marines. Octavian's ships resembled cavalry, now launching a charge, and now retreating, since they could attack or draw off as they chose, while Antony's were like heavy infantry, warding off the enemy's efforts to ram them, but also striving to hold them with their grappling-hooks. Each fleet in turn gained the advantage over the other: the one would dart in against the rows of oars which projected from the ships' sides and break the blades, while the other fighting from its higher decks would sink its adversaries with stones and ballistic missiles. At the same time each side had its weaknesses. Antony's ships could do no damage to the enemy as they approached: Octavian's, if they failed to sink a vessel when they had rammed it, would find the odds turned against them once they were grappled.

For a long while the struggle was evenly poised and neither side could gain the upper hand anywhere, but the end came in the following way. Cleopatra, whose ship was riding at anchor behind the battle lines, could not endure the long hours of uncertainty while the issue hung in the balance: both as a woman and as an Egyptian she found herself stretched to breaking-point by the agony of the suspense, and the constant and unnerving effort of picturing victory or defeat. Suddenly she made her choice—to flee—and made the signal for the others, her own subjects. So when her ships immediately hoisted their sails and stood out to sea, a favourable wind having luckily got up, Antony supposed that they were turning tail, not on Cleopatra's orders, but out of fear because they felt themselves to have been defeated, and so he followed them.

At this, dismay and confusion spread to the rest of Antony's men, and they re-solved likewise to take whatever means of escape lay open. Some raised their sails, while others threw the turrets and heavy equipment overboard to lighten the vessels and help them to get away. While they were thus engaged, their opponents again attacked: they had not pursued Cleopatra's fleeing squadron, because they themselves had not taken sails aboard and had put out prepared only for a naval battle. This meant that there were many ships to attack each one of Antony's, both at long range and alongside. The result was that the struggle took many forms on both sides and was carried on with the greatest ferocity. Octavian's soldiers battered the lower parts of the ships from stem to stern, smashed the oars, broke off the rudders, and, climbing on to the decks, grappled with their enemies. They dragged down some, thrust others overboard, and fought hand to hand with others, since they now equalled them in numbers. Antony's men forced their attackers back with boat-hooks, cut them down with axes, hurled down stones and other missiles which had been prepared for this purpose, forced down those who tried to scale the ships' sides, and engaged all who came within reach. A witness of the battle might have compared it, if one can reduce the scale, to the spectacle of a number of walled towns or islands set close together being besieged from the sea. Thus one side strove to clamber up the sides of the ships, as it might be up a cliff or fortress, and brought to bear all the equipment which is needed for such an assault, while the others struggled to

This modern depiction of the Battle of Actium shows the high battle towers on Antony's huge ships. Octavian's and Agrippa's smaller and faster vessels gave them the advantage.

repel them, using all the weapons and tactics which are known to defenders.

Dio Cassius, *Roman History: The Reign of Augustus,* trans. Ian Scott-Kilvert. New York: Penguin, 1987, pp. 58–60.

Augustus Amasses Great Power

In 27 B.C., the Senate conferred on Octavian the title Augustus, "the revered one." He was already in the process of consolidating numerous powers once held by separate republican officials and groups, and, eventually, as explained here by Dio Cassius, the government did almost nothing without his approval.

In this way the power of both people and senate passed entirely into the hands of Augustus, and from this time [January 27 B.C.] there was, strictly speaking, a monarchy; for monarchy would be the truest name for it. . . . Now, the Romans so detested the title "monarch" that they called their emperors neither dictators nor kings nor anything of this sort. Yet, since the final authority for the government devolves upon them, they needs must be kings. The offices established by the laws, it is true, are maintained even now, except that of censor; but the entire direction and administration is absolutely in accordance with the wishes of the one in power at the time. And yet, in order to preserve the appearance of having this authority not through their power but by virtue of the laws, the emperors have taken to themselves all the offices (including the titles) which under the Republic possessed great power with the consent of the people— with the exception of the dictatorship. Thus, they very often become consuls, and they are always styled proconsuls whenever they are outside the *pomerium* [official jurisdiction of the capital]. The title *imperator* [originally "victorious military commander"; later "emperor"] is held by them for life, not only by those who have won victories in battle but also by all the rest, to indicate their absolute power, instead of the title "king" or "dictator." These latter titles they have never assumed since they fell out of use in the constitution, but the actuality of those offices is secured to them by the appellation *imperator*. By virtue of the titles named, they secure the right to make levies, collect funds, declare war, make peace, and rule foreigners and citizens alike everywhere and always—even to the extent of being able to put to death both *equites* and senators inside the *pomerium*— and all the other powers once granted to the consuls and other officials possessing independent authority; and by virtue of holding the censorship they investigate our lives and morals as well as take the census, enrolling some in the equestrian and senatorial orders and removing others from these orders according to their will. By virtue of being consecrated in all the priesthoods and, in addition, from their right to bestow most of them upon others, as well as from the fact that, even if two or three persons rule jointly, one of them is *pontifex maximus* [high priest of the state religion], they hold in their own hands supreme authority over all matters both profane and sacred. The tribunician power, as it is called, which once the most influential men used to hold, gives them the right to nullify [veto] the effects of the measures taken by any other official, in case they do not approve, and makes their persons inviolable; and if they appear to be wronged in even the slightest degree, not merely by deed but even by word, they may destroy the guilty party as one accused, without a trial. . . .

Augustus did not enact all laws on his sole responsibility, but some of them he brought before the popular assembly in advance, in order that, if any features caused displeasure, he might learn it in time and correct them; for he encouraged everybody whatsoever to give him advice, in case anyone could think of any improvement in them, and he accorded them great freedom of speech; and he actually changed some provisions. Most important of all, he took as advisers for periods of six months the consuls (or the other consul, when he himself also held the office), one of each of the other kinds of officials, and fifteen men chosen by lot from the remainder of the senatorial body, so that it was his custom to communicate proposed legislation after a fashion through these to all the other senators. For although he brought some matters before the whole senate, he generally followed this course, considering it better to take under preliminary advisement in a leisurely fashion most matters, and especially the most important ones, in consultation with a few; and sometimes he even sat with these men in trials. The senate as a body, it is true, continued to sit in judgment as before, and in certain cases transacted business with embassies and envoys from both peoples and kings; and the people and the plebs, moreover, continued to come together for the elections; but nothing was actually done that did not please Caesar. At any rate, in the case of those who were to hold office, he himself selected and nominated some; and though he left the election of others in the hands of the people and the plebs, in accordance with the ancient practice, yet he took care that no persons should hold office who were unfit or elected as the result of factious combinations or bribery.

Dio Cassius, *Roman History,* quoted in Naphtali Lewis and Meyer Reinhold, eds., *Roman Civilization, Sourcebook II: The Empire.* New York: Harper and Row, 1966, pp. 4–7.

Augustus Rebuilds Rome

Among the great accomplishments of Augustus's long reign was a mighty burst of urban renewal, especially in the capital, as described here by Suetonius in his second-century biography of Augustus.

Since the city was not adorned as befitted the majesty of the empire and was exposed to flood and fire, he so beautified it that he could justly boast that he had found it a city of brick and left it a city of marble, and he certainly made it safe for the future, so far as human foresight could provide.

He erected many public works foremost among them the following: his Forum, with the Temple of Mars the Avenger; the Sanctuary of Apollo on the Palatine; and the Temple of Jupiter the Thunderer on the Capitol. His reason for building the Forum was the increase in the number of people and lawsuits, which seemed to call for still a third Forum, since two were no longer adequate. . . . He vowed the Temple of Mars when he undertook the war of Philippi to avenge his father [i.e., defeated Caesar's assassins at Philippi, in Greece]; accordingly, he decreed that in it the senate should deliberate on wars and requests for triumphs, from it men on their way to the provinces with military commands should be escorted, and to it victors on their return should bring the tokens of their triumphs. He erected the Sanctuary of Apollo in that part of his abode on the Palatine for which the soothsayers declared that the god had shown his desire by striking it with lightning; and he joined to it colonnades with Latin and Greek libraries, and when he was getting to be an old man it was there that he often held meetings of the senate or certified the panels of jurors. He dedicated the temple to Jupiter the Thunderer. . . .

He constructed some works too in the name of others—his grandsons, his wife, and his sister—such as the colonnade and basilica of Gaius and Lucius, the colonnades of Livia and Octavia, and the theater of Marcellus. More than that, he often urged other prominent men to adorn the city with new monuments or to restore and embellish old ones, each according to his means. And many works were erected at that time by many men: for example, the Temple of Hercules and the Muses by

Marcius Philippus, the Temple of Diana by Lucius Cornificius, the Hall of Liberty by Asinius Pollio, the Temple of Saturn by Munatius Plancus, a theater by Cornelius Balbus, an amphitheater by Statilius Taurus, and by Marcus Agrippa in particular many magnificent structures.

He divided the area of the city into districts and neighborhoods and arranged that the former should be under the charge of annual magistrates selected by lot and the

Augustus financed improvements on the Temple of Jupiter on the Capitoline hill (below) and erected the Temple of Mars the Avenger (right) in the Augustan Forum.

latter under captains elected by the people of the respective neighborhoods. To guard against fires he devised a system of stations of night watchmen [the *vigiles,* who combined fire-fighting and policing duties] and to control the floods he widened and cleared out the bed of the Tiber, which had for some time been filled with rubbish and narrowed by jutting buildings. Further, to make the approach to the city easier from every direction, he personally undertook to rebuild the Flaminian Road as far as Ariminum and assigned the rest of the highways to men who had been honored with triumphs to pave out of their spoils money.

He restored sacred edifices which had gone to ruin through lapse of time or had been destroyed by fire and adorned both these and the other temples with most lavish gifts; for example, in a simple donation he deposited in the shrine of Jupiter Capitolinus 16,000 pounds of gold and precious stones and pearls worth 50,000,000 sesterces.

Suetonius, *Lives of the Twelve Caesars,* quoted in Naphtali Lewis and Meyer Reinhold, eds., *Roman Civilization, Sourcebook II: The Empire.* New York: Harper and Row, 1966, pp. 67–69.

Augustus Boasts of His Deeds

In the last year of his reign (A.D. 14), Augustus composed the Res gestae, *a list of his accomplishments, and had it posted throughout the Empire. In these excerpts, he glosses over his ruthless rise to power and concentrates on positive events and deeds, including ending the civil wars, receiving the title "father of the country" and other honors, and generously distributing money by various means to the people.*

Below is a copy of the accomplishments of the deified Augustus by which he brought the whole world under the empire of the Roman people, and of the moneys expended by him on the state and the Roman people, as inscribed on two bronze pillars set up in Rome.

At the age of nineteen, on my own initiative and my own expense, I raised an army by means of which I liberated the Republic, which was oppressed by the tyranny of a faction [i.e., Mark Antony and his allies]. For which reason the senate, with honorific decrees, made me a member of its order in the consulship of Gaius Pansa and Aulus Hirtius, giving me at the same time consular rank in voting, and granted me the *imperium.* It ordered me as propraetor, together with the consuls, to see to it that the state suffered no harm. Moreover, in the same year, when both consuls had fallen in war, the people elected me consul and a triumvir for the settlement of the commonwealth.

Those who assassinated my father [Julius Caesar] I drove into exile, avenging their crime by due process of law; and afterwards when they waged war against the state, I conquered them twice on the battlefield.

I waged many wars throughout the whole world by land and by sea, both civil and foreign, and when victorious I spared all citizens who sought pardon. Foreign peoples who could safely be pardoned I preferred to spare rather than to extirpate. About 500,000 Roman citizens were under military oath to me. Of these, when their terms of service were ended, I settled in colonies or sent back to their own municipalities a little more than 300,000, and to all of these I allotted lands or granted money as rewards for military service. I captured 600 ships, exclusive of those which were of smaller class than triremes. . . .

In my fifth consulship I increased the number of patricians, by order of the people and the senate. Three times I revised the roll of senators. And in my sixth consulship, with Marcus Agrippa as my colleague, I conducted a census of the people. I performed the *lustrum* after an interval of forty-two years. At this *lustrum* 4,063,000 Roman citizens were recorded. Then a second time, acting alone, by virtue of the consular power, I completed the taking of the census in the consulship of Gaius Censorinus and Gaius Asinius. At this *lustrum* 4,233,000 Roman citizens were recorded. And a third time I completed the taking of the census in the consulship of Sextus Pompeius and Sextus Appuleius, by virtue of the consular power and with my son Tiberius Caesar as my colleague. At this *lustrum* 4,937,000 Roman citizens were recorded. By new legislation which I sponsored I restored many traditions of our ancestors which were falling into desuetude in our generation; and I myself handed down precedents in many spheres for posterity to imitate. . . .

To the Roman plebs I paid 300 sesterces apiece in accordance with the will of my father; and in my fifth consulship I gave each 400 sesterces in my own name out of the spoils of war; and a second time in my tenth consulship I paid out of my own patrimony a largess of 400 sesterces to every individual; in my eleventh consulship I made twelve distributions of food out of grain purchased at my own expense; and in the twelfth year of my tribunician power for the third time I gave 400 sesterces to every individual. These largesses of mine reached never less than 250,000 persons. In the eighteenth year of my tribunician power and my twelfth consulship I gave sixty *denarii* to each of 320,000 persons of the urban plebs. And in my fifth consulship I gave out of the spoils of war 1,000 sesterces apiece to my soldiers settled in colonies. This largess on the occasion of my triumph was received by about 120,000 persons in the colonies. In my thirteenth consulship I gave sixty *denarii* apiece to those of the plebs who at that time were receiving public grain; the number involved was a little more than 200,000 persons.

I reimbursed municipalities for the lands which I assigned to my soldiers in my fourth consulship, and afterwards in the consulship of Marcus and Gnaeus Lentulus the augur. The sums involved were about 600,000,000 sesterces which I paid for Italian estates, and about 260,000,000 sesterces which I paid for provincial lands. I was the first and only one to take such action of all those who up to my time estab-

Erected in 28 B.C., Augustus's mausoleum was the largest tomb in the Roman world. His wife, Livia, was buried there as well.

lished colonies of soldiers in Italy or in the provinces. And afterwards, in the consulship of Tiberius Nero and Gnaeus Piso, and likewise of Gaius Antistius and Decimus Laelius, and of Gaius Calvisius and Lucius Passienus, and of Lucius Lentulus and Marcus Messalla, and of Lucius Caninius and Quintus Fabricius, I granted bonuses in cash to the soldiers whom after the completion of their terms of service I sent back to their municipalities; and for this purpose I expended about 400,000,000 sesterces.

Four times I came to the assistance of the treasury with my own money, transferring to those in charge of the treasury 150,000,000 sesterces. And in the consul-

ship of Marcus Lepidus and Lucius Arruntius I transferred out of my own patrimony 170,000,000 sesterces to the soldiers' bonus fund, which was established on my advice for the purpose of providing bonuses for soldiers who had completed twenty or more years of service.

From the year in which Gnaeus Lentulus and Publius Lentulus were consuls, whenever the provincial taxes fell short, in the case sometimes of 100,000 persons and sometimes of many more, I made up their tribute in grain and in money from my own grain stores and my own patrimony. . . .

In my sixth and seventh consulships, after I had put an end to the civil wars, having attained supreme power by universal consent, I transferred the state from my own power to the control of the Roman senate and people. For this service of mine I received the title of Augustus by decree of the senate, and the doorposts of my house were publicly decked with laurels, the civic crown was affixed over my doorway, and a golden shield was set up in the Julian senate house, which, as the inscription on the shield testifies, the Roman senate and people gave me in recognition of my valor, clemency, justice, and devotion. After that time I excelled all in authority, but I possessed no more power than the others who were my colleagues in each magistracy.

When I held my thirteenth consulship, the senate, the equestrian order, and the entire Roman people gave me the title of "father of the country" and decreed that this title should be inscribed in the vestibule of my house, in the Julian senate house, and in the Augustan Forum on the pedestal of the chariot which was set up in my honor by decree of the senate. At the time I wrote this document I was in my seventy-sixth year.

Augustus Caesar, *Res gestae*, in William G. Sinnigen, ed., *Sources in Western Civilization: Rome.* New York: Free Press, 1965, pp. 104–108, 112–13.

Horace Advocates Moderation

Another of Augustus's major achievements was encouraging patronage of literature, *which enjoyed a golden age during his reign. Prominent among the Augustan poets was Horace (65–8 B.C.), who left behind this very wise advice about how to enjoy a stress-free life.*

You will live best by not going to extremes. By following the policy of the Golden Mean you will avoid envy for excessive wealth and the degradations of poverty. Too much prominence and wealth are attended by the greatest dangers; for when the fall comes, it is all the harder. All is change; life is full of ups and downs; nothing ever remains the same. Therefore, be hopeful when in trouble, anxious when prosperous. There is always a silver lining in the offing. Trouble cannot last forever, for nothing remains the same. Apollo is the god of plague, but also of music. Be brave in difficulties, cautious in prosperity. . . .

Peace and contentment is everyone's prayer. This cannot be bought with wealth. Political power and wealth will not drive away the cares of the mind. He lives well who lives on a little, undisturbed by fear or greed. Life is short. Why then should we aim at so much? You cannot escape yourself by travelling from place to place. Care follows you wherever you go, swifter than the wind. Life is full of change; nothing is perfect in every respect. Be happy now, don't worry about the future. Learn to smile at misfortune. No one can have everything. You have herds of animals and wealth. To me fate has granted a small estate, the inspiration of the Greek Muse, and scorn for the envious crowd.

Horace, *Odes,* quoted in Meyer Reinhold, *Essentials of Greek and Roman Classics.* Great Neck, NY: Barron's, 1946, pp. 307–309.

Virgil Recalls a Peaceful Past Age

Perhaps the greatest of the Augustan poets was Virgil (70–19 B.C.), author of Rome's national epic, the Aeneid. *Virgil is also famous for his* Georgics, *poems glorifying rustic rural life. In this excerpt from the second* Georgic, *he recalls the peace and plenty of the dimly remembered era before Rome knew war and the ills it causes.*

O happy beyond measure the tillers of the soil, if they but knew their blessings, on whom, far from the clash of arms, the earth most justly showers an easy livelihood from her soil! Even if no high mansion with proud portals pours forth from every room a mighty wave of men coming to pay their respects in the morning; even if men do not gape at pillars inlaid with lovely tortoise-shell, or at tapestries embroidered with gold, or at Corinthian bronzes; even if white wool is not dyed with oriental purple; even if the pure olive oil they use is not spoiled with perfume, yet they enjoy sleep without worry, and a life that cannot bring disillusionment but rather one that is rich in varied treasures, and peace in their broad farms, and grottoes, natural lakes, cool valleys, the lowing of cattle, and gentle slumber beneath a tree. Pastures are there and the haunts of wild game, and youth is hardy in toil and accustomed to simple fare; there the rites of the gods are observed and reverence for age survives; Justice took her last steps among these as she left the earth. . . .

But the farmer upturns the earth with his curved plow; this is his year-long toil, and thus he feeds his country and little grandchildren, his herds of cattle and bullocks that have served him well. Nor is there any halt throughout the year to the abundance of fruits or offspring of flocks or sheaves of grain, and his furrows are ever piled high with harvest and his granaries are filled to overflowing. When

Virgil, Rome's most renowned poet, recites verses to his patron, Gaius Maecenas.

winter comes, the Sicyan olives are pressed by the mills, the pigs return well fed on acorns, the woods produce wild strawberries, and autumn drops her varied fruits, and high up on sunny rocks mellow grapes are ripened. Meanwhile, sweet children hang about his lips, his chaste household preserves its purity, the cows' udders hang full of milk, and the fat kids in the luxuriant meadow butt against each other locking horn with horn. The master himself celebrates the festal days; stretched on the grass, while about a fire in their midst his comrades wreath the bowl, he pours libation and invokes thee, O Bacchus [god of wine and fertility], and for the shepherds of his flock he holds a contest of throwing the swift javelin at a mark on an elm tree, and they bare their hardened bodies for the rustic wrestling match.

This is the life the ancient Sabines once cherished; so, too, Remus and his brother [Romulus, Rome's founder]; thus, surely, brave Etruria waxed strong, and Rome became the fairest thing on earth, and encircled together her seven hills with a wall. Yea, before the power of the Cretan kings and before impious mankind fed on slaughtered oxen, this was the life that was led on earth in the Golden Age of Saturn. Yea, not yet had they heard the blast of trumpet, not yet the ring of swords placed on hard anvils.

Virgil, *Georgics*, quoted in Naphtali Lewis and Meyer Reinhold, eds., *Roman Civilization, Sourcebook II: The Empire*. New York: Harper and Row, 1966, pp. 21–23.

Smitten by Love

One of the more common themes of Augustan Age poetry was love; Roman readers were accustomed to poets' varied expressions of happy and unhappy love. In this charming example, Propertius (ca. 50–ca. 17 B.C.) tells how a woman can, in a sense, send out a group of cupids to smite her beloved and send him hurrying home to her.

Yesterday night, my light, when I was roving drunk
And had no servants to lead me along,
A crowd of little boys met me (I do not know
How many—fear stopped me counting them).
I saw that some were carrying little torches, others
Arrows, and a few had cords to tie me up.
But they were naked. Said a naughtier one of them
'Arrest this man. You know him well by now.
This was the one the angry woman hired us for.'
And as he spoke a noose was round my neck.
Then one said 'Push him into the middle', and another
'He thinks we're not Gods. He must die!
She's been expecting you for hours on end, but you,
Ungrateful lout, seek someone else's door.
When she's untied the Sidon snood she wears at night
And opened wide her drowsy eyes,
Fragrance will waft around you, not of Arabian grass

But made by the hands of Love himself.
Now free him, brothers. Now he promises
    true love,
And look, we've now come to the house as
    ordered'
And with this, putting on my cloak again,
    they said to me
'Go now and learn to stay at home of
    nights.'

Quoted in Peter Washington, ed., *The Roman Poets*. New York: Knopf, 1997, p. 135.

Augustus's Death and Legacy

When Augustus died in A.D. *14, the Roman nation was gripped by an enormous and sincere outpouring of grief and regret. Most Romans felt that he had led them away from the chaos and uncertainty of the past and into an age of peace and harmony. This moving passage from Dio Cassius's history begins with the great man on his deathbed in the town of Nola, south of Rome.*

He sent for his associates, and told them of all that he wanted to be done. Finally he declared, 'I found Rome built of clay: I leave it to you in marble.' In this saying he was not referring literally to the state of the buildings, but rather to the strength of the empire. And when he asked them for some applause, as comic actors do at the end of a mime, he was in fact mocking very aptly the whole life of man.

So on the nineteenth day of August, the very day on which he had first become consul, Augustus passed away. He had lived for seventy-five years, ten months and twenty-six days—he had been born on the twenty-third of September—and had been sole ruler, reckoning from the time of his victory at Actium, for forty-four years, less thirteen days. . . .

The body of Augustus was conveyed from Nola by the most prominent men of each city in succession. When it reached the neighbourhood of Rome, the knights received it into their charge and carried it by night into the city. . . .

After this his funeral took place. A couch was made of ivory and gold and spread with a pall of purple and gold. Beneath the covering his body was hidden in a coffin; above it a wax effigy, clad in triumphal dress, was displayed. This image was carried from the palace by the officials who had been appointed for the following year; another one of gold was borne from the Senate-house, and yet a third was placed on a triumphal chariot. Behind these were conveyed the images of Augustus's ancestors, of his deceased relatives, except for that of Julius Caesar, because he had been ranked among the demi-gods, and finally those of the other Romans of the past who had distinguished themselves in some way, beginning with Romulus himself. . . .

The whole Senate was present and walked in the funeral procession. So too did the equestrian order, their wives, the Praetorian Guard [the emperor's personal bodyguards] and indeed virtually all who were in Rome at the time. When the bier had been placed on the pyre in the Campus Martius, all the priests marched around it first, then came the knights, not only those who were to be senators but the others as well, and then the infantry of the Praetorian Guard circled it at a run and threw on to it all the triumphal decorations which any of them had ever received from the emperor for an act of valour. After this the centurions took torches, again in accordance with a senatorial decree, and set fire to the pyre from below. So it was consumed, and an eagle released from it flew aloft to bear the emperor's spirit to heaven. When these ceremonies had been completed, all the others departed, but Livia remained on the spot for five days, attended by the most distinguished of the knights; then

At Augustus's funeral, a soldier releases an eagle to symbolize the flight of the emperor's soul to heaven.

she had his bones gathered up and placed in his tomb. . . .

The Romans felt his death as a great loss, both for these reasons and for others besides. By dint of combining monarchy with democracy, he saved their freedom for them and at the same time established order and security, so that they were delivered alike from the lack of authority which prevails in a democracy and from the excess of it in a tyranny, and could live in a state of freedom enjoyed with moderation and under a monarchy which held no terrors for them; they were subjects of royalty without being slaves, and citizens of a democracy without suffering discord.

If any of them remembered Augustus's deeds during the civil wars, they attributed them to the pressure of circumstances. They judged it right to base their view of his disposition on what he did after he had come into the undisputed possession of supreme power, for here in truth there was an immense contrast. Anyone who examines his actions in detail can confirm this. But to sum them up briefly, I may say that he resolved the strife between the rival factions, remodelled the system of government in such a way as to equip it with the maximum of power and greatly strengthened it. For this reason, even if an occasional deed of violence did occur, such as is apt to happen in exceptional situations, it would be fairer to lay the blame on the circumstances rather than on him.

Dio Cassius, *Roman History: The Reign of Augustus,* trans. Ian Scott-Kilvert. New York: Penguin, 1987, pp. 245–47, 255–56.

The Home and Family Life

As in modern Western society, the home and family were the cornerstones of ancient Roman life. "What is there more holy, what is there more carefully fenced round with every description of religious respect, than the house of every individual citizen?"[1] asked the great first-century B.C. orator and statesman Cicero. For "house," Cicero used the Latin word *domus,* which could mean not only a physical dwelling but also the family.

One must be careful, however, not to equate the ancient Roman family strictly with the nuclear family as it is defined today (father, mother, and children). The Latin word *familia,* which is frequently translated today as "family," is more precisely rendered as "household," which could have several fairly broad meanings. Indeed, a Roman household might and often did feature a father, mother, and children. But it was not necessarily relationship by blood that made the mother and children part of the household; rather, they belonged to the *familia* because they were subject to the authority of its male head, the paterfamilias, the presiding father figure. That authority, which allowed him to rule family members according to his own desires, needs, and whims, was known as *patria potestas.*

A Roman family might also be extended. As the late scholar Harold Johnston put it, the household might include "adopted sons, married or unmarried, with their wives, sons, unmarried daughters, and even remoter descendants (always through males), yet they made but one *familia* in the eyes of the Romans."[2] As long as they remained under the authority of the paterfamilias, all such relatives were *alieno iuri subjecti,* or "dependent." Only he was *sui iuris,* or "independent." As such, he decreed if a family member should be punished or forgiven, decided who would be educated and to what degree, and arranged marriages for sons, daughters, nieces, nephews, and grandchildren.

An even wider meaning of the Roman household included the family slaves, the father's clients (people who did him favors in return for his legal or financial protection), all family possessions, and even the family's heritage (the tombs of deceased relatives and statues and other images of them) and private religious worship (including the household gods). It is no wonder, then, that

Cicero called a Roman's household "holy." "Here," he wrote, "are his altars, here are his hearths, here are his household gods. Here all his sacred rites, all his religious ceremonies are preserved."[3]

To a Roman, therefore, family and home often had a more reverent meaning than is common today. The Roman household was also more steeped in tradition and had a more structured and rigid framework. It is within this framework that love, marriage, divorce, child rearing, education, slaves, and other family matters must be considered.

Notes

1. Cicero, *On His House,* in C.D. Yonge, trans., *The Orations of Marcus Tullius Cicero.* London: George Bell, 1891, p. 182.
2. Harold W. Johnston, *The Private Life of the Romans.* New York: Cooper Square, 1973, p. 27.
3. Cicero, *On His House,* p. 182.

Dangers of Apartment Living

The most common form of housing in Roman cities was the insula, *or apartment block, featuring tenements ranging from three to seven stories in height. As described by the first-century A.D. satirist Juvenal, these mostly wooden buildings were often prone to damage by fire and collapse.*

We live in a city shored up, for the most part, with gimcrack

    Stays and props: that's how our landlords arrest

The collapse of their property, papering over great cracks

    In the ramshackle fabric, reassuring the tenants

They can sleep secure, when all the time the building

    Is poised like a house of cards. I prefer to live where

Fires and midnight panics are not quite such common events.

    By the time the smoke's got up to your third-floor apartment

(And you still asleep) your heroic downstairs neighbour

    Is roaring for water, and shifting his bits and pieces to safety.

If the alarm goes at ground-level, the last to fry

Will be the attic tenant, way up among the nesting

Pigeons with nothing but tiles between himself and the weather.

Juvenal, *Satires*, published as *The Sixteen Satires*, trans. Peter Green. New York: Penguin, 1974, p. 94.

Rooms and Shops for Rent

The ground floors of the insulae *often housed shops, small bathhouses, and other businesses. This is a surviving rental ad for a small apartment building in the town of Pompeii.*

FOR RENT
from August 13, with a 5-year lease
on the property of Julia Felix,
daughter of Spurius:
the elegant Venus Baths,
streetfront shops and booths,
and second-story apartments.

Quoted in Jo-Ann Shelton, ed., *As The Romans Did: A Sourcebook in Roman Social History.* New York: Oxford University Press, 1988, p. 65.

A Wealthy Country Villa

Next to the imperial palaces, the most impressive and comfortable Roman homes were the country villas of the well-to-do. Here, from a letter to a friend named Gallus, the first-century A.D. *nobleman Pliny the Younger describes his villa at Laurentum, on the sea-coast a few miles south of Rome's port city, Ostia.*

The villa is spacious enough for my needs, and the upkeep is not expensive. In the first part of it the entrance room is plain but not mean. Next there are colonnades [rows of columns] that come together in a form very much like the letter D, enclosing a small but pleasant area. This affords an excellent retreat in bad weather, as it is protected by windows, and much more by the overhanging roof. Beyond the middle of this there is an attractive inner court, and next a very handsome dining room which runs out towards the shore and is gently washed by the last lappings of the breakers whenever the sea is stirred up by the southwest wind. On every side this room has folding doors or equally huge windows, and so it affords a view from the sides and the front over three different seascapes. From the rear you see the inner court, the portico, and the enclosed area, then another portico, then the entrance room, the woods, and the far-distant mountains.

To the left of this dining room, somewhat recessed, is a large salon, then a second smaller one, one of whose windows faces east, the other west, also affording a view of the sea but a more unstudied one. The angle formed by the projection of this room and the dining room retains and increases the warmth of the very clear sunlight. This serves as a winter retreat, and also as a gymnasium for my household; here there are no winds except those which bring unsettled weather, and it is not until the fair weather is gone that the place loses its usefulness. Attached to the angle is another chamber with a bay window, whose windows admit sun all day long. Set in the wall of this room is a closet like a bookcase containing books that should be reread, not merely read. Attached to this is a bedroom connected to a passageway with a hollow floor and walls fitted with pipes from which it receives hot air circulated in all directions at a healthful temperature. The rest of this side of the house is reserved for the use of the slaves and freedmen, most of the rooms being elegant enough to accommodate guests.

On the other side is a very charming bedroom. Then another room, which can serve as a large bedroom or a small dining room, gets a good deal of light from the sun and a good deal from the reflection of the sea. Beyond this is a bedroom with an antechamber, suitable for summer use because of its height and also for winter use because it is sheltered and protected from all winds. Another bedroom and anteroom are joined to this one by a common wall.

Next comes the spacious and expansive cold room of the baths, in the opposite walls of which are two bath tubs curving outward as if forced out of the wall; these are quite roomy, when you consider how near the sea is. Adjacent are the anointing room, the furnace room, and also the steam room; then come two small cham-

A modern artist's reconstruction depicts the exterior of Pliny the Younger's summer villa at Tifernum.

bers, tasteful rather than sumptuous. Attached to these is a splendid warm pool, where one may swim and have a view of the sea. Close by is the ball court, which receives the very hot afternoon sun.

At this point there rises a tower which contains two apartments on the ground floor, the same number above, and in addition has a view far out to sea and commanding a long stretch of coast and very charming villas. There is also a second tower containing a bedroom with eastern and western exposure. Behind this is a wine closet and a grain storeroom, and on the floor below a dining room where one hears only a gentle and faint crashing sound when the sea is stormy; it overlooks the garden and the promenade which surrounds the garden.

The promenade is bordered with box trees [a type of evergreen] and with rosemary where box trees are missing; for the box grows well in the part which is sheltered by the buildings but withers where it is exposed to the sky, the wind, and the spray of the sea, however far away it is. Adjacent to the inner side of the promenade is a soft shady path, soft and yielding even to bare feet. The garden is thickly planted with mulberry and fig trees, for which the soil here is especially favorable, though not so suitable for others. There is a dining room here which, though removed from the sea, enjoys a view not inferior to one over the sea. Round the rear of it run two apartments whose windows overlook the entrance of the villa and another garden, lush and in country style.

Next, a covered gallery extends, almost large enough for a public structure. It has windows on both sides, more on the side facing the sea, fewer on the garden side, there being one here for every two on the other side. When the day is fair and serene, these are all kept open; but if it is windy, those on the side where the wind is gentle are kept open without discomfort. Before the covered gallery is a terrace perfumed with violets. The warmth is intensified by the reflection of the sun beating on the gallery, which both absorbs the sun's heat and checks and keeps off the northeast wind; and it is as warm in front as it is cool in the rear. In the same manner it checks the southwest wind, and thus it breaks the force of and halts winds blowing from any direction. This is the charm of this spot in the winter; but it is greater in the summer. For in the morning the terrace, and in the afternoon the nearest part of the promenade and garden, are made comfortably shady by it, and as the days grow longer or shorter, the shade that is cast is now shorter, now longer in one place or the other. The covered gallery itself is then shadiest when the sun is hottest and falls directly on the roof. In addition, when the windows are open, westerly breezes come in and blow through, and it never becomes close with stale and stagnant air.

At the head of the terrace and the gallery is a garden apartment, my favorite, really my favorite, for I had it constructed myself. It contains a sun parlor, one side of which has a view of the terrace, the other of the sea, and both are exposed to the sun;

and also a bedroom with a view of the covered gallery from its folding doors and of the sea from a window. Opposite the center wall is my retreat, very neatly recessed, which by its glazed windows and by opening or drawing the curtains can be joined to or shut off from the bedroom. It contains a couch and two chairs. Below is the sea, behind are villas, above are woods. These varied views can be seen from the windows either separately or in one panorama. Adjoining the retreat is a chamber for sleeping and napping. Neither the voices of the servants nor the murmur of the sea, nor even the fury of storms penetrate this, nor lightning, nor even daylight, unless the windows are open. The explanation of this deep and perfect solitude is an intervening passageway which separates the walls of the bedroom from the garden, and so every sound is absorbed by the empty space between. Attached to the bedroom is a very small heating apparatus, which through a tiny window lowers or raises the temperature as required. Next come a chamber and antechamber which reach out to the sun and catch the first rays of its rising and even retain it in the afternoon, though receiving it at an angle. When I retire to this apartment, I fancy myself far away even from my own villa, and I take particular pleasure in it especially at the Saturnalia [a religious holiday celebrated in December], when the remaining parts of the house resound with the license and the festive shouting of those days, for I don't hinder their festivities, and they don't disturb my studies.

Among these conveniences and pleasures there is one drawback—lack of running water, but there are wells, or rather springs, for they are on the surface. And the nature of this coast is quite remarkable, for wherever you dig, you at once encounter water, pure and not even slightly spoiled by the nearness of the sea. The nearby forests afford an abundant supply of fuel; all other necessities are supplied by the town of Ostia. Indeed, a man living modestly would find the village adequate, which is separated from my villa by only one other villa. In this village there are three public bathing establishments, a great convenience if perchance a sudden arrival or a rather short stay makes it inadvisable to heat up the bath at home.

Pliny the Younger, *Letters,* quoted in Naphtali Lewis and Meyer Reinhold, eds., *Roman Civilization, Sourcebook II: The Empire.* New York: Harper and Row, 1966, pp. 248–51.

Proper Layout of a Farming Villa

The luxurious villa described by Pliny was designed as a residence and retreat. Farming villas, on the other hand, served as the focus of a farming estate. The first-century A.D. estate owner Lucius Junius Columella penned this description of what he saw as the best design for such a structure.

The size of a villa or housing structure should be determined by the total area of the farm; and the villa should be divided into three sections: one section resem-

A well-to-do Roman farm featured a central villa, often divided into separate apartments.

promenades should have a southern exposure so that they may receive both the maximum of sun in the winter and the minimum in the summer.

Now in the farmhouse part of the villa there should be a large kitchen with a high ceiling, and for two reasons: so that the wood beams may be secure against the danger of fire, and so that household slaves may conveniently stop by here during every season of the year. The best plan will be to construct the cells for unchained slaves facing south. For those in chains let there be an underground prison, as healthful as possible, and let it be lighted by many narrow windows which are built so far from the ground that they cannot be reached with a hand.

Columella, *On Agriculture,* quoted in Jo-Ann Shelton, ed., *As The Romans Did: A Sourcebook in Roman Social History.* New York: Oxford University Press, 1988, p. 73.

bling a city home [for the landowner], one section like a real farmhouse [for the workers and livestock], and the third section for storing farm products.

The landowner's section of the villa should be further divided into a winter apartment and a summer apartment. The winter bedrooms should face southeast and the winter dining rooms due west. The summer bedrooms, on the other hand, should face due south, but the dining rooms for this same season should face southeast. The baths should be turned toward the northwest so that they may be lighted from midday until evening. The

Fond Praise for a Roman Father

The paterfamilias, or father figure, in a Roman household usually garnered much respect from other family members. Such respect was not restricted to wealthy households, as shown by this passage by the poet Horace, who fondly remembers his father, the poor son of a freedman (freed slave).

If my character is flawed by a few minor faults, but is otherwise decent and moral, if you can point out only a few scattered blemishes on an otherwise immaculate surface, if no one can accuse me of greed or of sordidness or of profligacy, if I live a virtuous life, free of defilement (pardon, for a moment, my self-praise), and if I am to my friends a good friend, my father deserves all the credit. For although he was a poor man, with only an infertile plot of land, he was not content to send me to Flavius's school [the school in his home town] which the burly sons of burly centurions [army officers] attended, carrying their book-bags and writing tablets slung over their left shoulders and paying their few pennies on the Ides [paying the teachers at the middle of the month]. My father had the courage to take his boy to Rome, to have him taught the same skills which any equestrian or senator would have his sons taught. If anyone had seen my clothing or the slaves that attended me, as is the custom in a large city, he would have thought that my expenses were being paid for from an ancestral estate. But my paedagogus [slave who accompanied a boy to school] my absolutely incorruptible guardian, was my father who accompanied me to school. Need I say more? He kept me pure, which is the highest level of virtue, not only from every vice, but even from any insinuation of vice. He didn't make these sacrifices because he worried that someone might criticize him if I became a crier [a man who recited the news in public] or, like him, a money-collector; nor would I have complained if he hadn't taken me to Rome. But as it is now, he deserves from me unstinting gratitude and praise. I could never be ashamed

of such a father, nor do I feel any need, as many people do, to apologize for being a freedman's son.

Horace, *Satires,* quoted in Jo-Ann Shelton, ed., *As The Romans Did: A Sourcebook in Roman Social History.* New York: Oxford University Press, 1988, p. 19.

An Arranged Marriage

Many Roman marriages were arranged by fathers, uncles, or other relatives. In this letter, Pliny the Younger answers a friend who has asked him to help find a suitable husband for the friend's niece.

You ask me to look out for a husband for your brother's daughter, a responsibility which I feel is very rightly mine; for you know how I have always loved and admired him as the finest of men, and how he influenced my early years by his advice and encouraged me to become worthy of his praise. You could not entrust me with anything which I value or welcome so much, nor could there be any more befitting duty for me than to select a young man worthy to be the father of Arulenus Rusticus's grandchildren.

I should have had a long search if Minicius Acilianus were not at hand, as if he were made for us. He loves me as warmly as one young man does another (he is a little younger than I am), but respects me as his elder, for he aspires to be influenced and guided by me, as I was by you and your brother. His native place is Brixia [in northern Italy], one of the towns in our part of Italy which still retains intact much of its honest simplicity along with the rustic virtues of the past. His father is Minicius Macrinus, who chose to remain a leading member of the order of knights because he desired nothing higher; the deified Emperor Vespasian would have raised him to praetorian rank, but he has always steadfastly preferred a life of honest obscurity to our status—or our struggles to gain it. His maternal grandmother, Serrana Procula, comes from the town of Patavium [now Padua] whose reputation you know; but Serrana is a model of propriety even to the Patavians. His uncle, Publius Acilius, is a man of exceptional character, wisdom and integrity. You will in fact find nothing to criticize in the whole household, any more than in your own.

Acilianus himself has abundant energy and application, but no lack of modesty. He has held the offices of quaestor, tribune and praetor with great distinction, thus sparing you the necessity of canvasing on his behalf. He has a frank expression, and his complexion is fresh and high-coloured; his general good looks have a natural nobility and the dignified bearing of a senator. (I think these points should be mentioned, as a son of just return for a bride's virginity.) I am wondering whether to add that his father has ample means; for if I picture you and your brother for whom we are seeking a son-in-law, I feel no more need be said; but in view of the prevailing habits of the day and the laws of the country which judge a man's income

Some Roman husbands and wives developed close, loving unions that stood the test of time.

to be of primary importance, perhaps after all his something which should not be omitted. Certainly if one thinks of the children of the marriage, and subsequent generations, the question of money must be taken into account as a factor influencing our choice.

Pliny the Younger, *Letters*, published as *The Letters of the Younger Pliny*, trans. Betty Radice. New York: Penguin, 1969, pp. 47–48.

Respect for His Departed Wife

Although many Roman marriages were arranged, husbands and wives often developed respectful and loving relationships.

Part of the evidence for this consists of tomb epitaphs such as this one, found at Rome and dating from the second century B.C.

Stranger, I have only a few words to say. Stop and read them—This is the unlovely tomb of a lovely woman. Her parents named her Claudia. She loved her husband with all her heart. She bore two sons; one of these she leaves here on earth, the other she has already placed under the earth. She was charming in speech, yet pleasant and proper in manner. She managed the household well. She spun wool—I have spoken. Go on your way.

Quoted in Jo-Ann Shelton, ed., *As The Romans Did: A Sourcebook in Roman Social History.* New York: Oxford University Press, 1988, p. 45.

A Long and Happy Marriage

This anonymous epitaph, dating from the first century B.C., might have been written by a man named Quintus Vespillo for his wife, Turia. Whoever the author was, it is clear that he and his wife shared a deep love, which he claims is rare in his day.

Marriages of such long duration, not dissolved by divorce, but terminated by death alone, are indeed rare. For our union was prolonged in unclouded happiness for forty-one years. Would that our long marriage had come to its final end by *my* death, and that *I* as the older—which was more just—had yielded to fate.

These sculpted figures of a Roman couple are part of the monument that marked their gravesite.

Why recall your natural qualities, your modesty, deference, affability, your amiable disposition, your faithful attendance to household duties, your enlightened religion, your unassuming elegance, the modest simplicity of your attire? Need I speak of your attachment to your kindred, your affection for your family—when you cherished my mother as you did your own parents—you who share countless other virtues with Roman matrons who cherish their fair name? These qualities which I claim for you are your own; few have possessed the like and been able to hold on to and maintain them; the experience of men teaches us how rare they are. . . .

[When I was unfairly condemned and hunted during the civil war] you helped my escape by selling your jewels and turning over to me all your gold and the pearls removed from your person; and thereupon the household furnished money; and deceiving the guards of our opponents, you made my absence comfortable. . . .

When all the world was again at peace and the Republic reestablished, peaceful and happy days followed for us. We longed for children, which an envious fate denied us. . . .

Would that our time of life had permitted our union to endure until I, the older, had passed away—which was more just—and that you might perform for me the last rites, and that I might have departed, leaving you behind, with a daughter to replace me in your widowhood.

By fate's decree your course was run before mine. You left me the grief, the longing for you, the sad fate to live alone. . . .

The conclusion of this oration will be that you have deserved all, and that I remain with the chagrin of not being able to repay you all. Your wishes have always been my supreme law; and whatever it will

be granted to me to do in addition, in this I shall not fail.

I pray that your *Manes* [personal household spirits] may assure and protect your repose.

Quoted in Naphtali Lewis and Meyer Reinhold, eds., *Roman Civilization, Sourcebook I: The Republic.* New York: Harper and Row, 1966, pp. 485–87.

A Secret Love Affair

Despite many loving and faithful marriages, adultery was as common in ancient Rome as it is in modern society. The noted Augustan poet Ovid (43 B.C.–A.D. 17), who was known for his witty, charming verses, gives the following advice to his secret mistress in carrying on right under her husband's nose at a party.

Your Husband? Going to the same dinner as us? I hope it chokes him.
So I'm only to gaze at you, darling? Play gooseberry while another man enjoys your touch?
You'll lie there snuggling up to him? He'll put his arm round your neck whenever he wants?
No wonder Centaurs [mythical creatures who were half-man and half-horse] fought over Hippodamia when the wedding wine began to flow.
I don't live in the forest nor am I part horse but I find it hard to keep my hands off you.
However here's my plan. Listen carefully. Don't throw my words of wisdom to the winds.

Arrive before him—not that I see what good arriving first will do but arrive first all the same.

When he takes his place on the couch and you go to join him looking angelic, secretly touch my foot.

This engraving presents an idealized portrait of the Augustan poet Ovid.

Watch me for nods and looks that talk and unobserved return my signals

in the language of eyebrows and fingers with annotations in wine.

Whenever you think of our love-making stroke that rosy cheek with your thumb.

If you're cross with me, darling, press the lobe of your ear

but turn your ring round if you're pleased with anything I say or do.

When you feel like cursing your fool of a husband touch the table as if you were praying.

If he mixes you a drink, beware—tell him to drink it himself, then quietly ask the waiter for what you want.

I'll intercept the glass as you hand it back and drink from the side you drank from.

Refuse all food he has tasted first—it has touched his lips.

Don't lean your gentle head against his shoulder and don't let him embrace you

or slide a hand inside your dress or touch your breasts. Above all don't kiss him.

If you do I'll cause a public scandal, grab you and claim possession.

I'm bound to see all this. It's what I shan't see that worries me—the goings on under your cloak.

Don't press your thigh or your leg against his or touch his coarse feet with your toes.

I know all the tricks. That's why I'm worried. I hate to think of him doing what I've done.

We've often made love under your cloak, sweetheart, in a glorious race against time.

You won't do that, I know. Still, to avoid all doubt don't wear one.

Encourage him to drink but mind—no kisses. Keep filling his glass when he's not looking.

If the wine's too much for him and he drops off we can take our cue from what's going on around us.

When you get up to leave and we all follow move to the middle of the crowd.

You'll find me there—or I'll find you so touch me anywhere you can.

But what's the good? I'm only temporizing. Tonight decrees our separation.

Tonight he'll lock you in and leave me desolated at your door.

Then he'll kiss you, then go further, forcing his right to our secret joy.

But you *can* show him you're acting under duress. Be mean with your love— give grudgingly—in silence.

He won't enjoy it if my prayers are answered. And if they're not, at least assure me you won't.

But whatever happens tonight tell me tomorrow you didn't sleep with him— and stick to that story.

Ovid, *Amores*, quoted in Bernard M.W. Knox, ed., *The Norton Book of Classical Literature*. New York: W.W. Norton, 1993, pp. 728–31.

The Correct Way to Raise Children

In general, Roman parents maintained strict discipline in raising children. The urbane first-century A.D. *playwright, essayist, and courtier Seneca the Younger gives the following advice on the subject, warning that too much coddling will spoil a child.*

It is of the utmost importance that children be raised in the correct manner even if this means harsh discipline. We must be careful not to allow them to have fits of anger, but we must also be careful not to stifle their individual personalities. . . . Unlimited freedom creates an intractable personality, total repression produces an abject personality. Praise lifts the spirit and makes a child self-confident, but too much praise makes him insolent and bad-tempered. We must therefore steer a middle course when raising a child, sometimes checking him back, sometimes spurring him on. . . . Don't let him whine and pester you for treats; give rewards only for good deeds or for promised good behavior. When he is thrust into competition with children of his own age, don't let him sulk or become angry. . . . When he wins or does something laudable, he should be praised, but not allowed to become excessively elated, for joy leads to exultation, and exultation leads to a swollen head and an inflated opinion of oneself. We should allow a certain amount of leisure, but never let this develop into idleness and sloth, and never let the child become accustomed to a soft and easy life. . . . For the child who has been denied nothing, whose tears an anxious mother always dried, . . . this child will be unable to cope with the harsh realities of life.

Seneca, *Essay on Anger*, quoted in Jo-Ann Shelton, ed., *As The Romans Did: A Sourcebook in Roman Social History*. New York: Oxford University Press, 1988, pp. 31–32.

A Modest Meal at Home

As is true today, the types of foods the Romans consumed depended on various factors, including their financial means. Well-to-do households could afford more meat, while poorer families relied more on vegetables. In one of his famous epigrams, the first-century A.D. poet and humorist Martial describes a typical meal in his modest home.

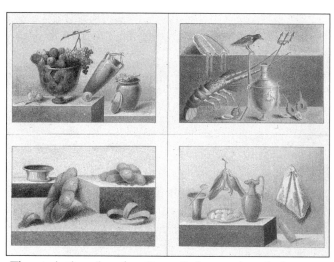

These paintings found at Pompeii show various foods eaten by the ancient Romans.

If the thought of a gloomy dinner at home depresses you, Toranius, you can go hungry with me. If it's your habit to take a snack beforehand, you won't lack for cheap Cappadocian lettuces and smelly leeks, chopped tunny [fish] will lurk in halves of egg. A green cabbage-sprout fresh from the chilly garden will be served on a black plate for your oily fingers to handle, and a sausage lying on snow-white porridge and pale beans with ruddy bacon. If you wish for the bounties of dessert, you will be offered withering [preserves of] grapes and pears that bear the name of Syrian and chestnuts roasted in a slow fire, produce of cultured Naples. The wine you will make good by drinking it. If after all this Bacchus [god of wine] perchance rouses an appetite, as his way is, fine olives will come to your aid, recently borne by the branches of Picenum, and hot chickpeas and warm lupins [beans]. A modest little meal (who can deny it?).

Martial, *Epigrams,* ed. and trans. D.R. Shackleton Bailey. 3 vols. Cambridge, MA: Harvard University Press, 1993, vol.1, pp. 419–21.

An Enlightened View of Slaves

Among the most important members of the average Roman household were the slaves. They were usually treated as inferiors and sometimes physically or sexually abused; however, at least some Romans disdained such cruelty, as evidenced by this now famous letter by Seneca.

I'm glad to hear, from these people who've been visiting you, that you live on friendly terms with your slaves. It is just what one expects of an enlightened, cultivated person like yourself. 'They're slaves,' people say. No. They're human beings. 'They're slaves.' But they share the same roof as ourselves. 'They're slaves.' No, they're friends, humble friends. 'They're slaves.' Strictly speaking they're our fellow-slaves, if you once reflect that fortune has as much power over us as over them.

This is why I laugh at those people who think it degrading for a man to eat with his slave. Why do they think it degrading? Only because the most arrogant of conventions has decreed that the master of the house be surrounded at his dinner by a crowd of slaves, who have to stand around while he eats more than he can hold, loading an already distended belly in his monstrous greed until it proves incapable any longer of performing the function of a belly, at which point he expends more effort in vomiting everything up than he did in forcing it down. And all this time the poor slaves are forbidden to move their lips to speak, let alone to eat. The slightest murmur is checked with a stick; not even accidental sounds like a cough, or a sneeze, or a hiccup are let off a beating. All night long they go on standing about, dumb and hungry, paying grievously for any interruption.

The result is that slaves who cannot talk before his face talk about him behind his back. The slaves of former days, however, whose mouths were not sealed up like this, who were able to make conversation not only in the presence of their master but actually with him, were ready to bare their necks to the executioner for him, to divert on to themselves any danger that threatened him; they talked at dinner but under torture they kept their mouths shut. It is just this high-handed treatment which is responsible for the frequently heard saying, 'You've as many enemies as you've slaves.' They are not our enemies when we acquire them; we make them so. . . .

I don't want to involve myself in an endless topic of debate by discussing the treatment of slaves, towards whom we Romans are exceptionally arrogant, harsh and insulting. But the essence of the advice I'd like to give is this: treat your inferiors in the way in which you would like to be treated by your own superiors. And whenever it strikes you how much power you have over your slave, let it also strike you that your own master has just as much power over you. 'I haven't got a master,' you say. You're young yet; there's always the chance that you'll have one. . . .

A bust of Seneca, playwright, philosopher, and adviser to the emperor Nero.

'He's a slave.' But he may have the spirit of a free man. 'He's a slave.' But is that really to count against him? Show me a man who isn't a slave; one is a slave to sex, another to money, another to ambition; all are slaves to hope or fear. I could show you a man who has been a Consul who is a slave to his 'little old woman', a millionaire who is the slave of a little girl in domestic service. I could show you some highly aristocratic young men who are utter slaves to stage artistes. And there's no state of slavery more disgraceful than one which is self-imposed. So you needn't allow yourself to be deterred by the snobbish people I've been talking about from showing good humour towards your slaves instead of adopting an attitude of arrogant superiority towards them. Have them respect you rather than fear you.

Seneca, *Letters,* published as *Seneca: Letters From a Stoic,* trans. Robin Campbell. New York: Penguin, 1969, pp. 90, 93, 95.

The Improving Lot of Slaves

Some of the emperors, notably in the second century, were nearly as enlightened as Seneca was about slavery, and passed various laws banning cruel treatment of slaves. Such laws by Hadrian (ruled 117–138) were recorded in this passage from a fourth-century history of uncertain authorship.

He prohibited the killing of slaves by their owners and ordered that they should be sentenced by judges if they deserved it. He prohibited the sale of a male or female slave to a pimp or gladiatorial trainer without cause being given. . . . Workhouses for slaves and freedmen he abolished. He divided public baths between the sexes. In cases where a slave-owner had been murdered in his house he ruled that not all the slaves should be put to the torture but only those who were in a position to have some knowledge through having been in the vicinity.

Augustan History, published as *Lives of the Later Caesars, The First Part of the* Augustan History, *with Newly Compiled Lives of Nerva and Trajan,* trans. Anthony Birley. New York: Penguin, 1976, p. 77.

A Slave Becomes a Member of the Family

In many Roman homes, trusted slaves were treated as members of the family, and on occasion a master actually freed a slave and adopted him or her as his child. This tomb inscription, found in Greece, records the death of an adopted former slave at age sixteen.

Here lies Vitalis, slave of Gaius Lavius Faustus and also his son, a slave born in his home. He lived sixteen years, [was] a clerk at the Aprian shop [?], popular with the public, but snatched away by the gods. I beg your pardon, wayfarers, if I ever gave short measure to make more profit for my father. I beg you by the gods above and

Roman slaves stand on an auction block. Some will end up in households, others on farming estates.

below to take good care of my father and mother. And farewell.

Quoted in Naphtali Lewis and Meyer Reinhold, eds., *Roman Civilization, Sourcebook II: The Empire.* New York: Harper and Row, 1966, p. 266.

A Master Killed by His Slaves

Regardless of the kindness of some slave owners and periodic legislation to lessen cruelty to slaves, many masters continued to treat their slaves badly; such owners lived perpetu-

ally under the shadow of possible retaliation. In this letter, Pliny the Younger tells how one man's slaves turned on him.

This horrible affair demands more publicity than a letter—Larcius Macedo, a senator and ex-praetor, has fallen a victim to his own slaves. Admittedly he was a cruel and overbearing master, too ready to forget that his father had been a slave, or perhaps too keenly conscious of it. He was taking a bath in his house at Formiae when suddenly he found himself surrounded; one slave seized him by the throat while the others struck his face and hit him in the chest and stomach and—shocking to say—in his private parts. When they thought he was dead they threw him on to the hot pavement, to make sure he was not still alive. Whether unconscious or feigning to be so, he lay there motionless, thus making them believe that he was quite dead. Only then was he carried out, as if he had fainted with the heat, and received by his slaves who had remained faithful, while his concubines ran up, screaming frantically. Roused by their cries and revived by the cooler air he opened his eyes and made some movement to show that he was alive, it being now safe to do so. The guilty slaves fled, but most of them have been arrested and a search is being made for the others. Macedo was brought back to life with difficulty, but only for a few days; at least he died with the satisfaction of having revenged himself, for he lived to see the same punishment meted out as for murder. There you see the dangers, outrages, and insults to which we are exposed. No master can feel safe because he is kind and considerate; for it is their brutality, not their reasoning capacity, which leads slaves to murder masters.

Pliny the Younger, *Letters*, published as *The Letters of the Younger Pliny*, trans. Betty Radice. New York: Penguin Books, 1969, pp. 100–101.

Entertainment and Leisure Activities

The Romans followed or copied numerous aspects of Greek culture, including the Olympian gods and their myths, architectural styles, and epic poetry and other literary forms. One area in which the Romans largely rejected Greek custom was the basic nature of leisure pursuits and entertainment, especially sports and games. For one thing, the Romans came to enjoy big, violent displays more than the Greeks. Although the Greeks pioneered chariot races, their version was on a much smaller scale than the races the Romans held in huge stone amphitheaters such as Rome's mighty Circus Maximus. Also, the Greeks did not stage gladiatorial bouts and wild animal shows, in which humans and beasts fought to the death.

An even more crucial difference between Greek and Roman entertainment and sports events, one often overlooked today, concerned who participated in these activities. Greek social tradition encouraged and glorified athletic participation by citizens of all walks of life; hence the huge popularity of the Olympic Games and similar sports competitions throughout the Greek world. In contrast, most Romans had little or no desire to participate in such activities. They enjoyed watching public games, especially violent ones, but it was considered socially unacceptable for them actually to take part. Usually the performers were slaves, criminals, actors, and others viewed in Roman society as disreputable.

The Circus Maximus, Rome's largest racetrack, underwent many improvements over the centuries. Its stone seats were not completed until the early first century A.D.

This attitude, which seems prudish and elitist to us today, was based partly on pride. Traditionally, the Romans were a conservative, austere people who were deeply proud of their military abilities and accomplishments and viewed defeat on the battlefield as the ultimate disgrace. To Romans, losing an athletic competition was uncomfortably similar to losing on the battlefield. "No Roman could stand the risk of losing such an individual test, of looking inferior in public," classical scholar David Young writes. Moreover, most Romans found the Greek custom of competing in the nude disturbing. To appear naked in full view of the enemy, Young adds, "would have made Roman blood run cold." [1]

It is not surprising, therefore, that the Romans saw running, throwing, swimming, and other such exercises as more appropriate for military training than friendly competition. And many popular Roman leisure activitics were those in which people were spectators or otherwise passive. Among free, respectable Romans, those who engaged in track and field events, weight lifting, mountain climbing, and other active pursuits were always greatly outnumbered by those who attended the public games or lounged in the public baths.

Notes
1. D.C. Young, *The Olympic Myth of Greek Amateur Athletics.* Chicago: Ares, 1984, p. 173.

Thrills and Spills on the Racetrack

Chariot racing was perhaps the most popular of all Roman entertainments. This tract by the fifth-century Roman poet Sidonius Apollinaris is a rare eyewitness account of a race in Rome's huge Circus Maximus, in which Sidonius's friend, the charioteer Consentius, was the victor.

The four team colors are clearly visible: white and blue, green and red. [The drivers wore tunics dyed in these colors. Each color represented a distinct racing organization, or faction, a private stable owned by a businessman, a *dominus factionis.*] Grooms are holding the heads and the bridles of the horses, . . . calming them with soothing pats and reassuring them with words of encouragement. Still the horses fret in the gates, lean against the starting barrier, and snort loudly. . . . They rear up, prance, and kick impatiently against the wood of the gates. A shrill blast of the trumpet, and the chariots leap out of the gates, onto the track. . . . The wheels fly over the ground, and the air is choked with the dust stirred up on the track. The drivers urge their horses with whips. Standing in the chariots, they lean far forward so that they can whip even the shoulders of the horses. . . . The chariots fly out of sight, quickly covering the long open stretch. . . . When they have come around the far turn, both the rival teams have passed Consentius, but his partner is in the lead. The middle teams concentrate now on taking the lead in the inside lane. [The drivers vied for the inside lane because the distance of position was somewhat shorter than in the outer lanes.] If the driver in front pulls his horses too far right toward the spectator stands, he leaves an opening on his left, in the inside lane. [The chariots raced counterclockwise, so that all the turns were to the left. They were also quite sharp—close to 180 degrees—making them very difficult to maneuver without veering off sideways and losing precious time.] Consentius, however, redoubles his efforts to hold back his horses and skillfully reserve their energy for the seventh and last lap. The others race full out, urging their horses with whip and voice. The track is moist with the sweat of both horses and drivers. . . . And thus they race, the first lap, the second, the third, the fourth. In the fifth lap, the leader is no longer able to withstand the pressure of his pursuers. He knows his horses are exhausted, that they can no longer respond to his demand for speed, and he pulls them aside. When the sixth lap had been completed and the crowd was already demanding that the prize be awarded, Consentius's opponents thought they had a very safe lead for the seventh and last lap, and they drove with self-confidence, not a bit worried about a move by Consentius. But suddenly he loosens the reins, plants his feet firmly on the floorboard, leans far over the chariot, . . . and makes his fast horses gallop full out. One of the other drivers tries to make a very sharp turn at the far post, feeling Consentius close on his heels, but he is unable to turn his four wildly excited horses, and they plunge out of control. Consentius passes him carefully. The fourth driver is enthralled by the cheers of the spectators and turns his galloping horses too far right toward the stands. Consentius drives straight and fast, and passes the driver who has angled out and only now, too late, begun to urge his horses with the whip. The latter pursues Consentius recklessly, hoping to overtake him. He cuts in sharply across the track. His horses lose their balance and fall. Their legs become tangled in the spinning chariot wheels and are snapped and broken. The driver is hurled headlong out of the shattered chariot which then falls on top of him in a heap of twisted wreckage. His broken and bloody body is still. [Sometimes other chariots crashed into the first to go down, a disaster known as a "shipwreck."] . . . And now the

Two chariots vie for the lead in a race held in the Circus Maximus. Drivers tried to hug the central spine of the track, since a circuit was slightly shorter in that lane.

emperor presents the palm branch of victory to Consentius.

Sidonius Apollinaris, *Poems,* quoted in Jo-Ann Shelton, ed., *As The Romans Did: A Sourcebook in Roman Social History.* New York: Oxford University Press, 1988, p. 351–52.

Epitaph for a Charioteer

Successful charioteers became huge celebrities in Rome. Martial wrote this epitaph for one of the greatest—Scorpus, who lived in the late first century A.D. and won 2,048 races.

I am Scorpus, the glory of the clamorous circus, your applause, Rome, and brief darling. Envious Lachesis [one of the three fates, she was thought to determine the length of life's thread] snatched me away ere my thirtieth year, but, counting my victories, believed me an old man.

Martial, *Epigrams,* ed. and trans. D.R. Shackleton Bailey. 3 vols. Cambridge, MA: Harvard University Press, 1993, vol. 2, p. 375.

A Charioteer's Illustrious Career

This inscription, found in Rome and dating from the second century A.D., celebrates the career of Diocles, one of the more successful drivers who appeared in the Circus Maximus. It was probably erected by some of his fans or fellow drivers.

Gaius Appuleius Diocles, charioteer of the Red Stable, a Lusitanian Spaniard by birth,

A charioteer holds the reins in one hand, a palm branch of victory in the other.

aged 42 years, 7 months, 23 days. He drove his first chariot in the White Stable, in the consulship of Acilius Aviola and Corellius Pansa [A.D. 122]. He won his first victory in the same stable, in the consulship of Manius Acilius Glabrio and Gaius Bellicius Torquatus [A.D. 129]. He drove for the first time in the Green Stable in the consulship of Torquatus Asprenas (for the second time) and Annius Libo [A.D. 125]. He won his first victory in the Red Stable in the consulship of Laenas Pontianus and Antonius Rufinus [A.D. 131].

Grand totals: He drove chariots for 24 years, ran 4,257 starts, and won 1,462 victories, 110 in opening races. In single-entry races he won 1,064 victories, winning 92 major purses, 32 of them (including 3 with six-horse teams) at 30,000 sesterces, 28 (including 2 with six-horse teams) at 40,000 sesterces, 29 (including 1 with a seven-horse team) at 50,000 sesterces, and 3 at 60,000 sesterces; in two-entry races he won 347 victories, including 4 with three-horse teams at 15,000 sesterces; in three-entry races he won 51 victories. He won or placed 2,900 times, taking 861 second places, 576 third places, and 1 fourth place at 1,000 sesterces; he failed to place 1,351 times. He tied a Blue for first place 10 times and a White 91 times, twice for 30,000 sesterces. He won a total of 35,863,120 sesterces. In addition, in races with two-horse teams for 1,000 sesterces he won three times, and tied a White once and a Green twice. He took the lead and won 815 times, came from behind to win 67 times, won under handicap 36 times, won in various styles 42 times, and won in a final dash 502 times (216 over the Greens, 205 over the Blues, 81 over the Whites). He made nine horses 100-time winners, and one a 200-time winner.

Quoted in Naphtali Lewis and Meyer Reinhold, eds., *Roman Civilization, Sourcebook II: The Empire.* New York: Harper and Row, 1966, pp. 230–31.

The Public Baths

One of the more popular pastimes in ancient Rome was attending the public baths, an activity that hundreds of thousands of people engaged in on a daily basis. This description of the interior of a large bath building is by the second-century A.D. Greek writer Lucian.

The building suits the magnitude of the site, accords well with the accepted idea of such an establishment, and shows regard for the principles of lighting. The entrance is high, with a flight of broad steps of which the tread is greater than the pitch, to make them easy to ascend. On entering, one is received into a public hall of good size, with ample accommodations for servants and attendants. On the left are the lounging rooms, also of just the right sort for a bath, attractive, brightly lighted retreats. Then, besides them, a hall, larger than need be for the purposes of a bath, but necessary for the reception of richer persons. Next, capacious locker rooms to undress in, on each side, with a very high and brilliantly lighted hall between them, in which are three swimming pools of cold water; it is finished in Laconian marble, and has two statues of white marble in the ancient style, one of Hygeia [goddess of health], the other of Aesculapius [god of healing and Hygeia's father].

On leaving this hall, you come into another which is slightly warmed instead of meeting you at once with fierce heat; it is oblong, and has an apse on each side. Next to it, on the right, is a very bright hall, nicely fitted up for massage, which has on each side an entrance decorated with Phrygian marble, and receives those who come in from the exercising floor. Then near this is another hall, the most beautiful in the world, in which one can

The spectacular entrance hall of the Baths of Caracalla, erected in the early third century.

stand or sit with comfort, linger without danger, and stroll about with profit. It also is refulgent with Phrygian marble clear to the roof. Next comes the hot corridor, faced with Numidian marble. The hall beyond it is very beautiful, full of abundant light and aglow with color like that of purple hangings. It contains three hot tubs.

When you have bathed, you need not go back through the same rooms, but can go directly to the cold room through a slightly warmed chamber. Everywhere there is copious illumination and full indoor daylight. . . . Why should I go on to tell you of the exercising floor and of the cloak rooms? . . . Moreover, it is beautified with all other marks of thoughtfulness—with two toilets, many exits, and two devices for telling time, a water clock that makes a bellowing sound and a sundial.

Lucian, *The Baths,* quoted in Naphtali Lewis and Meyer Reinhold, eds., *Roman Civilization, Sourcebook II: The Empire.* New York: Harper and Row, 1966, pp. 227–28.

The Growing Demand for Luxury

The Romans did not always have huge bathhouses like the one Lucian describes. In the early Republic, bathing facilities were mostly private and small. In this excerpt from one of his letters, Seneca describes a stay at the aging house that once belonged to the great general Scipio (who defeated Hannibal more than two centuries before), where he found himself comparing the tiny, spare bathroom

Scipio had used with the grandiose, luxurious bathhouses of his own time.

The tiny little bath [is] situated after the old-fashioned custom in an ill-lit corner, our ancestors believing that the only place where one could properly have a hot bath was in the dark. It was this which started in my mind reflections that occasioned me a good deal of enjoyment as I compared Scipio's way of life and our own. . . .

Who is there who could bear to have a bath in such surroundings nowadays? We think ourselves poorly off, living like paupers, if the walls are not ablaze with large and costly circular mirrors, if our Alexandrian marbles are not decorated with panels of Numidian marble, if the whole of their surface has not been given a decorative overlay of elaborate patterns having all the variety of fresco murals, unless the ceiling cannot be seen for glass, unless the pools into which we lower bodies with all the strength drained out of them by lengthy periods in the sweating room are edged with Thasian marble (which was once the rarest of sights even in a temple), unless the water pours from silver taps. And so far we have only been talking about the ordinary fellow's plumbing. What about the bath-houses of certain former slaves? Look at their arrays of statues, their assemblies of columns that do not support a thing but are put up purely for ornament, just for the sake of spending money. Look at the cascades of water splashing noisily down from one to the next. We have actually come to such

A reconstructed scene from a room in a small but elegant Roman bathhouse.

a pitch of choosiness that we object to walking on anything other than precious stones.

In this bathroom of Scipio's there are tiny chinks—you could hardly call them windows—pierced in the masonry of the wall in such a way as to let in light without in any way weakening its defensive character. Nowadays 'moth-hole' is the way some people speak of a bathroom unless it has been designed to catch the sun through enormous windows all day long, unless a person can acquire a tan at the same time as he is having a bath, unless he has views from the bath over countryside and sea.

The result is that bath-houses which drew admiring crowds when they were first opened are actually dismissed as antiquated as soon as extravagance has hit on any novelty calculated to put its own best previous efforts in the shade. There was a time when bath-houses were few and far between, and never in the least luxuriously appointed—and why should they have been, considering that they were designed for use, not for diversion, and that admission only cost you a copper? There were no showers in those days, and the water did not come in a continuous gush as if from a hot spring. People did not think it mattered then how clear the water was in which they were going to get rid of the dirt. . . .

'How primitive!' Such is some people's verdict on Scipio because he did not have extensive areas of glass to let the daylight into the perspiring room, because it was not a habit with him to stew in strong sunlight, letting the time go by until he was perfectly cooked in his own bathroom. 'What a sorry wretch of a man! He didn't know how to live! He'd take his bath in water that was never filtered and often cloudy, practically muddy in fact after any heavy rain.' Well, it did not make much difference to Scipio if this was the kind of bath he had; he went there to wash off sweat, not scent. And what do you think some people will say to this? 'Well, I don't envy Scipio; if that was the kind of bath he had all the time, it was a real exile's life that he was leading.'

Seneca, *Letters,* published as *Seneca: Letters from a Stoic,* trans. Robin Campbell. New York: Penguin, 1969, pp. 145–48.

A Dinner Invitation

Having friends over for dinner was a favorite pastime of Romans of all walks of life. In one of his epigrams, Martial re-creates the style of an invitation, which mentions not only the time and menu, but also the entertainment.

You will dine pretty well with me, Julius Cerealis; if you have no better engagement, come along. You will be able to keep the eighth hour [i.e., I will be serving dinner at eight]. We'll bathe together—you know how close I am to Stephanus' baths. First

Slaves serve the guests at a large dinner party in a well-to-do Roman home.

you'll be given lettuce (a good aperient) and strands cut from their parent leeks, next, an aged tunny [tuna fish], larger than a small mackerel, garnished with eggs and rue leaves. Other eggs, cooked in warm embers, will not be wanting, and a block of cheese congealed over a Velabran hearth, and olives that have felt the frosts of Picenum. So much for the hors d'oeuvres. You want to know the rest? I'll lie to make you come [i.e., let's pretend the menu is more appealing than it really is]: fish, collops [small pieces of meat], sow's udder, fat birds of the poultry yard and the marsh, things that even Stella as a rule serves only at a special dinner. I promise something more: I'll recite nothing to you, though *you* may read me your "Giants" on and on or your poems of the countryside, that rank next to immortal Virgil.

Martial, *Epigrams,* ed. and trans. D.R. Shackleton Bailey. 3 vols. Cambridge, MA: Harvard University Press, 1993, vol. 3, p. 47.

The Artistry of a Juggler

In addition to literary recitations, the entertainment at more well-to-do dinner parties (as well as at public theatrical events) often included singers, dancers, wrestlers, and jugglers. Martial here describes the artistry of a juggler named Agathinus, who was able to toss and catch a shield with various parts of his body.

Nimble Agathinus, you play very dangerous games, but you will not manage to let your little shield fall. It follows you against your will, and returns through the air to sit on your foot or your back, your hair or your fingernail. Though the stage be slippery from a Corycian shower [a sprinkling of saffron] and swift south winds tear away the awning denied us, the neglected shield roams over the boy's heedless limbs; wind and water do not impair the artistry. Though you want to make a mistake, whatever you do, you cannot slip; skill is needed to make your shield fall.

Martial, *Epigrams,* ed. and trans. D.R. Shackleton Bailey. 3 vols. Cambridge, MA: Harvard University Press, 1993, vol. 2, p. 265.

A Roman Doggy Bag

It was customary for diners to take home their leftovers in a napkin, the equivalent of today's doggy bag. Here, Martial pokes fun at a guest who tried to make off with a whole meal.

Whatever is served, you sweep it up from this side and that: teats of sow's udder, rib of pork, a wood-cock meant for two, half a mullet and a whole pike, side of lamprey, leg of fowl, pigeon dripping with its gravy. When these have been secreted in a greasy cloth, they are handed to your boy to be taken home. As for us, we just recline, an idle throng. If you have any sense of decency, put back the dinner. I did not invite you for tomorrow, Caecilianus.

Martial, *Epigrams,* ed. and trans. D.R. Shackleton Bailey. 3 vols. Cambridge, MA: Harvard University Press, 1993, vol. 1, p. 161.

Public Recitations

Besides the private readings offered at some dinner parties, Romans attended public recitations of poetry and prose, although, as the refined lover of literature Pliny the Younger complains in one of his letters, these events attracted a limited audience.

This year has raised a fine crop of poets; there was scarcely a day throughout the month of April when someone was not giving a public reading. I am glad to see that literature flourishes and there is a show of budding talent, in spite of the fact that people are slow to form an audience. Most of them sit about in public places, gossiping and wasting their time when they could be giving their attention, and give orders that they are to be told at intervals whether the reader has come in and has read the preface, or is coming to the end of the book. It is not till that moment—and even then very reluctantly—that they come dawdling in. Nor do they stay very long, but leave before the end some of them trying to slip out unobserved and others marching, boldly out. And yet people tell how in our fathers' time the Emperor Claudius was walking on the Palatine when he heard voices and asked what was happening; on learning that Nonianus was giving a reading he surprised the audience by joining it unannounced. Today the man with any amount of leisure, invited well in advance and given many a reminder, either never comes at all, or, if he does, complains that he has wasted a day—just because he has not wasted it. The more praise and

Octavia, sister of Octavian, swoons during a poetry recitation given by Virgil.

honour then is due to those whose interest in writing and reading aloud is not damped by the idleness and conceit of their listeners.

Pliny the Younger, *Letters*, published as *The Letters of the Younger Pliny*, trans. Betty Radice. New York: Penguin Books, 1969, pp. 46–47.

The Art of Pantomime

Roman pantomimes were popular stage presentations in which actors and dancers acted out stories to music, much like modern ballets. This excellent description of a pantomime based on the myth called the Judgment of Paris (in which a youth named Paris awards a golden apple to the most beautiful of three competing goddesses) comes from the imaginative, colorful second-century A.D. *novel,* The Golden Ass, *by Apuleius.*

The day appointed for the show was now at hand. As I was led to the theatre, a crowd of people cheering in procession attended me. During the preliminaries of the show, devoted to mimic dances by performers on the stage, I was posted before the gate. . . . The curtain was raised, the backcloths were folded away, and the stage was set.

A mountain of wood had been constructed with consummate workmanship to represent the famous mountain which the poet Homer in his song called Mount Ida. It was planted with thickets and live trees, and from its summit it disgorged river-water from a flowing fountain installed by the craftsman's hands. One or two she-goats were cropping blades of grass, and a youth was acting out control of the flock. He was handsomely dressed to represent the Phrygian shepherd Paris, with exotic garments flowing from his shoulders, and his head-crowned with a tiara [crown] of gold. Standing by him appeared a radiant boy, naked except for a youth's cloak draped over his left shoulder; his blonde hair made him the cynosure [center of attention] of all eyes. Tiny wings of gold were projecting from his locks, in which they had been fastened symmetrically on both sides. The herald's staff and the wand which he carried identified him as Mercury. He danced briskly forward, holding in his right hand an apple gilded with gold leaf, which he handed to the boy playing the part of Paris. After conveying Jupiter's command with a motion of the head, he at once gracefully withdrew and disappeared from the scene. Next appeared a worthy-looking girl, similar in appearance to the goddess Juno, for her hair was ordered with a white diadem, and she carried a sceptre. A second girl then burst in, whom you would have recognized as Minerva. Her head was covered with a gleaming helmet which was itself crowned with an olive-wreath; she bore a shield and brandished a spear, simulating the goddess's fighting-role.

After them a third girl entered, her beauty visibly unsurpassed. Her charming, ambrosia-like complexion intimated that she represented the earlier Venus when that goddess was still a maiden. She vaunted her unblemished beauty by appearing naked and unclothed except for a thin silken garment veiling her entrancing lower parts. An inquisitive gust of air would at one moment with quite lubricious affection blow this garment aside, so that when wafted away it revealed her virgin bloom; at another moment it would wantonly breathe directly upon it, clinging tightly and vividly outlining the pleasurable prospect of her lower limbs. The goddess's appearance offered contrasting colours to the eye, for her body was dazzling white, intimating her descent from heaven, and her robe was dark blue, denoting her emergence from the sea.

Each maiden representing a goddess was accompanied by her own escort. Juno was attended by Castor and Pollux, their heads covered by egg-shaped helmets prominently topped with stars; these Castors were represented by boys on stage. The maiden playing this role advanced with restrained and unpretentious movements to the music of an Ionian flute playing a range of tunes; with dignified motions she promised the shepherd to bestow on him the kingship of all Asia if he awarded her the prize for beauty. The girl whose appearance in arms had revealed her as Minerva was protected by two boys who were the comrades in arms of the battle-goddess, Terror and Fear; they pranced about with swords unsheathed, and behind her back a flutist played a battle-tune in the Dorian mode [a popular musical style]. He mingled shrill whistling notes with deep, droning chords like a trumpet-blast, stirring the performers to lively and supple dancing. Minerva with motions of the head, menacing gaze, and writhing movements incisively informed Paris that if he awarded her the victory for beauty, her aid would make him a doughty fighter, famed for the trophies gained in wars.

In addition to pantomimes, Roman theatricals included stage plays. This sculpture shows actors wearing masks in the Greek style.

But now Venus becomingly took the centre of the stage to the great acclamation of the theatre, and smiled sweetly. She was surrounded by a throng of the happiest children; you would have sworn that those litle boys whose skins were smooth and milk-white were genuine Cupids who had just flown in from sky or sea. They looked just the part with their tiny wings, miniature arrows, and the rest of their get-up, as with gleaming torches they lit the way for their mistress as though she were *en route* to a wedding-banquet. Next floated in charming children, unmarried girls, representing on one side the Graces [minor goddesses] at their most graceful, and on the other the Hours in all their beauty. They were appeasing their goddess by strewing wreaths and single blossoms before her, and they formed a most elegant chorus-line as they sought to please the Mistress of pleasures with the foliage of spring. The flutes with their many stops were now rendering in sweet harmony melodies in the Lydian mode. As they affectingly softened the hearts of the onlookers, Venus still more affectingly began gently to stir herself; with gradual, lingering steps, restrained swaying of the hips, and slow inclination of the head she began to advance, her refined movements matching the soft sounds of the flutes. Occasionally her eyes alone would dance, as at one moment she gently lowered her lids, and at another imperiously signalled with threatening glances. At the moment when she met the gaze of the judge, the beckoning of her arms seemed to hold the promise that if he preferred her over the other goddesses, she would present Paris with a bride of unmatched beauty, one like herself. There and then the Phrygian youth spontaneously awarded the girl the golden apple in his hand, which signalled the vote for victory.

Apuleius, *The Golden Ass,* trans. P.G. Walsh. Oxford: Oxford University Press, 1994, pp. 212–15.

An Outing on the Appian Way

Traveling, including long walking trips, was a pastime popular among Romans who had the time, money, and stamina. Following is the famous description of such a trip taken in 38 B.C. by the Roman poet Horace and some friends on the Appian Way (or Via Appia), the major roadway that ran for about 370 miles from Rome to the port of Brundisium, on Italy's eastern coast. According to Horace, the trip had its high points but large portions were difficult and uncomfortable.

When I left mighty Rome, I found bed and board in a modest inn at Aricia [a town about sixteen miles from Rome]. My companion was the rhetorician [speech teacher or orator] Heliodorus, far and away the most learned of the Greeks. Next we reached the Forum of Appius, swarming with sailors and knavish tavern-keepers. [The Forum of Appius was a town located about twenty-seven miles from Aricia. From Appius, travelers took a ferry boat across some marshes to reach the next stretch of road.] We felt lazy enough to cut

The Appian Way, on which Horace and his companions traveled. This stretch near Rome's main gate was lined with tombs, many designed to look like buildings.

this stretch in two, whereas travellers who gird up their loins take it in one go: the Appian Way is less tiring to those who are not in a hurry. There, by reason of the water, which was frightful, my stomach and I were on hostile terms and I waited with some impatience for my companions, who were dining.

Already the shadows of night were beginning to creep over the earth and stars were pinpointing the heavens. Then slaves bellowed at boatmen and boatmen at slaves: 'Heave to, here', 'You've got three hundred in'! 'Stop! that's enough.' After the fares had been collected and the mule harnessed, a whole hour went by. The cursed mosqui-

toes, the frogs of the marshland drove off sleep. Whereupon, after their fill of poor wine, a boatman and a passenger vied in singing of the girl each of them had left behind. At length, the weary passenger fell asleep and the lazy boatman unharnessed his mule and let it out to graze, tying its leading rein to a stone. Then he too started to snore away on his back. And it was already daylight when we found that the boat was not yet under way. So one of us, hot-headed fellow, jumped ashore and, with a stick cut from a willow, belaboured head and back of both mule and boatman. At last, upon the fourth hour, no earlier, we came ashore. We washed face and hands in thy waters, O Feronia [an ancient Italian goddess who had a spring dedicated to her at the point where the ferry ride ended]. Then, after, having had breakfast, we struggled along for three miles to reach the foot of [the town of Terracina], perched on its white rocks gleaming from afar.

Here the gallant Maecenas and Cocceius were to meet us, both sent as envoys to deal with important matters and both accustomed to bringing together divided friends. Here, too, I made use of a black ointment on my sore eyes. Meantime up came Maecenas and Cocceius, together with Fonteius Capito, a man of matchless perfection, so that Antony can have no closer friend. We were not sorry to leave Fundi [a town lying about thirteen miles beyond Terracina] and its praetor Aufidius Luscus, laughing at the knick-knacks with which that old clerk bedecked himself in his crazy vanity, laughing too at his bordered robe and his broad stripe and his pan of charcoal. Then, weary indeed, we made a long halt in the town of the Mamurrae [residents of the town of Formiae, about thirteen miles from Fundi], where Murena [a friend] provided us with lodging and Capito with board.

Dawn the next day was most delightful: for at Sinuessa [seventeen miles from

A modern illustration captures the bustle of the traffic on the Appian Way. People from many lands traveled along this roadway.

Formiae] we were joined by Plotius, Varius and Virgil. Earth has never borne purer souls, there is no man more attached to them than I. Oh! the embraces and the joy! So long as I have my senses, nothing will compare for me to the delight of friendship.

The little post-house close to the Campanian bridge [ten miles beyond Sinuessa] offered us the shelter of its roof, while the state purveyors dutifully provided wood and salt. Next, at the appointed time, our mules laid aside their panniers at Capua. Maecenas went off for exercise, while Virgil and I retired to sleep, for sport is the enemy of weary eyes and sore stomachs.

Our next stop was at the richly furnished villa of Cocceius, situated above the inns of Caudium. . . .

A merry company did we make over that meal. Thence we made our way [for a distance of eleven miles] straight to Beneventum, where, in his eagerness to please, our host, was nearly burned up while turning some lean thrushes over the fire. For Vulcan [Roman god of the forge] slipped out and the wandering flame spread through the old kitchen, rising to lick the very roof. Then you would have seen the starving guests and the trembling slaves grabbing the meal, and afterwards doing their best to put out the blaze.

Thenceforward Apulia was beginning to reveal its mountains, which I know so well, scorched by the Altino [a strong local wind] and over which we would never have been able to scramble, had we not found a welcome at a country house in the neighbourhood of Trivicum [about twenty-five miles from Beneventum], not without smoke that drew tears, for in the hearth were burning damp branches, leaves and all. There, in my complete stupidity, I waited until the middle of the night for a lying wench; however, sleep overcame me, impassioned as I still was; and, while I lay on my back, lustful dreams soiled me.

From that point we were taken 24 miles in Gallic carriages, to halt in a small town whose name cannot be put into verse, though it is easy enough to give some clues: the commonest of things, water, is sold there, but the local bread is quite magnificent, so much so that the wise traveller takes a quantity with him as he goes on his way, for at Carnusium the bread is as hard as stone, while there is not a jugful of water to be had in this town founded in bygone days by brave Diomedes [a mythical hero of the Trojan War who was said to have established several towns in Italy]. Here Varius sorrowfully took leave of his weeping friends.

Next we came to Rubi, very weary indeed, for we had gone a very long stage, with conditions made worse furthermore by the rain. The following day, the weather improved, but the track was even viler [i.e., the road was choked with mud] until we reached the walls of the little fishing-port of Barium. Then [the town of] Gnathia . . . gave us occasion to laugh and make pleasantry: for there people would have it that incense placed on the temple threshold melts without the need of fire. [Those who are gullible] may believe it; I do not, for I have learnt that the gods spend their time eternally at repose and that, if there are extraordinary phenomena produced by nature, it is not they who, to relieve their boredom, send these things down from their heavenly abode on high.

Brundisium is the end of this long tale and this long journey.

Horace, *Satires,* quoted in Raymond Chevallier, *Roman Roads,* trans. N.H. Field. Berkeley and Los Angeles: University of California Press, 1976, pp. 24–26.

Hunting to Keep Fit

Hunting was a popular activity in the Roman world, although large-scale hunts using horses and dogs were expensive and therefore a province of the affluent. One such country gentleman was the fourth-century orator and writer Quintus Aurelius Symmachus, who in a letter advocated hunting as a way for men, both young and old, to keep fit.

You are hunting—which shows that you are vigorous and healthy; and nothing pleases me more than that you keep yourselves fit by country sport. After that, I am delighted that your hunting has been so successful, that you can honour the gods and gratify your friends—the gods by nailing up antlers of stags and fangs of wild boars on the walls of their temples, your friends by sending them presents of game. I have no sympathy with the opinion that hunting is a slavish pursuit. Admirable as the literary style of the exponent of this view may have been, his own

moral obliquity hardly qualified him to respect as an authority on the good life. I would rather see you being countrymen with Atilius and pursuing tough sport than being seduced by literary precepts to the cult of soft living. This is the right occupation for men of your age. Young men should relax from their studies not in dicing, playing ball or trundling a hoop, but in exhausting spirited activity and in the enjoyment of exercising courage in a way that can do no harm. I shall encourage my boy to hunt as soon as he is old enough, even though he is my only son.

The time will come when old age weighs heavily on you and you will have to give up hunting. When that time comes, you can rightly talk of hunting in terms of slavery, for a man *is* a slave if, when his bodily strength goes, he refuses to avail himself of the respite from such strenuous exercise which old age affords.

Symmachus, *Letters,* quoted in J.P.V.D. Balsdon, *Life and Leisure in Ancient Rome.* New York: McGraw-Hill, 1969, p. 220.

Braving the Great Volcano

Although mountain climbing was not widely popular in the ancient Mediterranean world, some hardy individuals did pursue it. In his Geography, *the first-century* B.C. *Greek traveler Strabo tells how a few unusually brave climbers even ventured to the summit of Mt. Etna, a huge and active volcano in Sicily.*

Near the town of Centoripa is a small village called Etna, which takes in climbers and sends them on their way, for the ridge of the mountain begins here. Those who had recently climbed the summit told me that at the top was a level plain, some 20 stades in circumference, around which was a pile of ashes as high as the wall of a house, so that if anyone wished to get down into this plain he had to jump down from this wall. . . . Two of their party were courageous enough to venture into the plain of this crater, but since the sand on which they were walking was becoming hotter and deeper, they turned back and could not tell their friends who were watching anything more than these friends could see for themselves. They went on to say that as far as they could observe, many of the accounts about the crater are just stories, especially the tale about [the Greek philosopher] Empedokles, who is alleged to have leaped into the crater and as a clue to his fate left behind one of the brass sandals he wore. This sandal, my informants told me, was found a little way from the rim of the crater, as if it had been propelled by the force of the fire. But as a matter of fact this place cannot be approached or even seen, nor could anything be thrown into the crater because of the blast of air from the interior.

Strabo, *Geography*, quoted in Waldo E. Sweet, ed., *Sport and Recreation in Ancient Greece: A Sourcebook with Translations*. New York: Oxford University Press, 1987, p. 158.

At Home in the Water

As is true in coastal areas today, many Romans who lived near Mediterranean coasts enjoyed the beach and water sports, including boating and swimming. This passage by the first-century A.D. Roman writer Marcus Manilius describes a person swimming, wading, and floating, clearly someone at home in the water.

For just as the dolphin glides through the water on swift fins, now rising above the surface and now sinking to the depths, and piles up moving waves and sends them off in circles, just so will each person born under the sign of the Dolphin fly through the waves, raising one arm and then the other in slow arcs. At one moment one can hear the sound of the water as he strikes it, at another moment he will separate his arms under water, like an oar concealed by the water, and at another time he will enter the water in a vertical position and will pretend to swim when he is walking and pretending to have found a shallow place he will imitate a field on top of the water. Or he will rest his motionless limbs by bringing them to his back and sides; he does not depress the water but will float on top of the waves and will hang there, an entire boat without a rower.

Manilius, *On Astronomy*, quoted in Waldo E. Sweet, ed., *Sport and Recreation in Ancient Greece: A Sourcebook with Translations*. New York: Oxford University Press, 1987, p. 162.

Chapter

6

Gods and Religious Worship

Like most other peoples, both ancient and modern, the Romans were overall devoutly religious and believed in divine beings more powerful than themselves. "Most philosophers have affirmed the existence of the gods," the great first-century B.C. orator Cicero wrote. "And indeed, such an assertion is plausible and one to which we are all naturally inclined."[1] What made Roman society different than many others was its tolerance for a wide range of gods and religious views. Cicero described the religious debate of his day:

> Among those who assert gods exist there is such variety and conflict of opinions that it would be tedious to list them all. There are many different theories about the shapes in which the gods appear, about their homes and habitations, about the manner of their life, and all of these theories are the subject of constant dispute among philosophers.[2]

Indeed, in the last two centuries of the Republic and first two centuries of the Empire, the Romans repeatedly imported new gods and faiths from peoples across the Mediterranean world. From Asia Minor came Cybele, the "Mother Goddess"; from Egypt, Isis; from Persia, Mithras; from Syria, Atargatis; and so on. These deities took their place in Roman worship alongside those of the traditional Roman pantheon—the group of gods headed by Jupiter (the Greek Zeus)—as well as various formless spirits thought to inhabit the home and the fields.

All were widely accepted and respected by most Romans, although each person or group tended to worship only one or a select few on a regular basis.

Modern readers will immediately be struck by this cosmopolitan attitude toward the divine. Today's three major monotheistic faiths—Christianity, Judaism, and Islam—hold that all other deities and faiths but the one true god and faith are false, and advocate a single spiritual path. In contrast, the fourth-century Roman orator Symmachus wrote:

> The divine mind has distributed different guardians and different cults to different cities. . . . It is just that all worship should be considered as one. We

Public worship in Rome took place outside ornate temples like this one. No sacrifices or other ceremonies took place inside, so as to respect a god's privacy.

look at the same stars [and] the same world surrounds us. What difference does it make by what pains each seeks the truth? We can not attain to so great a secret by one road.[3]

This attitude explains how so many diverse religions could thrive at the same time in Roman society. For the most part they were not in competition or exclusivist, but part of a greater scheme in which many roads led to the same place. For the Romans, adopting this attitude was a matter not only of tolerance, but also, quite plainly, of practicality, since it allowed them to absorb and rule many and diverse subject peoples.

Notes
1. Cicero, *The Nature of the Gods*, trans. Horace C.P. McGregor. New York: Penguin, 1972, p. 69.
2. Cicero, *Nature of the Gods*, p. 69.
3. Quoted in Brian Tierney, ed., *The Middle Ages, Volume I: Sources of Medieval History*. New York: Knopf, 1973, pp. 23–24.

Rites and Duties of Roman Religion

This excerpt from Cicero's Laws *was intended to outline the religious institutions of an ideal state. It is valuable in that it lists the major rites of Roman worship in his own day, including sacrifice and religious festivals, as well as the various religious duties expected of priests and ordinary people.*

They shall approach the gods in purity, bringing piety and leaving riches behind. Whoever shall do otherwise, heaven itself will deal out punishment to him.

No one shall have gods to himself, either new gods or alien gods, unless recognized by the state. Privately they shall worship those gods whose worship they have duly received from their ancestors.

In cities they shall have shrines; they shall have groves in the country and homes for the *Lares* [household spirits].

They shall preserve the rites of their families and their ancestors.

They shall worship as gods both those who have always been regarded as dwellers in heaven, and also those [human heroes] whose merits have admitted them to heaven: Hercules, Liber, Aesculapius, Castor, Pollux, Quirinus; also those qualities through which an ascent to heaven is granted to mankind: Intellect, Virtue, Piety, Good Faith. To their praise there shall be shrines, but none for the vices.

They shall perform the established rites.

On holidays they shall refrain from lawsuits; these they shall celebrate together with their slaves after their tasks are done. Let holidays be so arranged as to fall at regularly recurring breaks in the year. The priest shall offer on behalf of the state the prescribed grains and the prescribed fruits; this shall be done according to prescribed rites and on prescribed days; likewise for other days they shall reserve the plenteous offerings of the milk and the offspring [sacrifices of liquids and animals]. And so that no violation of these customs shall take place, the priests shall determine the mode and the annual circuit of such offerings; and they shall prescribe the victims which are proper and pleasing to each of the gods.

The several gods shall have their several priests, the gods altogether their pontiffs [state priests] and the individual gods their flamens [special priests]. The Vestal Virgins shall guard the eternal fire on the public hearth of the city.

Those who are ignorant as to the methods and rites suitable to these public and private sacrifices shall seek instructions from the public priests. Of them there shall be three kinds: one to have charge of ceremonies and sacred rites; another to interpret those obscure sayings of soothsayers and prophets which shall be recognized by the senate and the people; and the interpreters of Jupiter the Best and Greatest, namely the public augurs, shall foretell the future from portents and auspices, and maintain their art. And the priests shall observe the omens in regard to vineyards and orchards and the safety of the people; those who carry on war or affairs of state shall be informed by them beforehand of the auspices and shall obey them; the priests shall foresee the wrath of the gods and yield to it; they shall observe flashes of lightning in fixed regions of the sky, and shall keep free and unobstructed the city and fields and their places of observation. Whatever an augur shall declare to be unjust, unholy, pernicious, or ill-omened shall be null and void; and whosoever yields not obedience shall be put to death.

The fetial priests shall be judges and messengers for treaties, peace and war,

A flamen, *a priest appointed to the service of a single deity, makes an offering at an altar.*

truces, and embassies; they shall make the decisions in regard to war.

Prodigies and portents [divine signs of coming events] shall be referred to the Etruscan soothsayers, if the senate so decree; Etruria [the old Etruscan homeland, located north of Rome] shall instruct her leading men in this art. They shall make expiatory offerings to whatever gods they decide upon, and shall perform expiations for flashes of lightning and for whatever shall be struck by lightning.

No sacrifices shall be performed by women at night except those offered for the people in proper form [i.e., the worship of Bona Dea, rites attended only by women]; nor shall anyone be initiated except into the Greek rites of Ceres, according to the custom.

Sacrilege which cannot be expiated shall be held to be impiously committed; that which can be expiated shall be atoned for by the public priests.

At the public games which are held without chariot races or the contest of body with body, the public pleasure shall be provided for with moderation by song to the music of harp and flute, and this shall be combined with honor to the gods.

Of the ancestral rites the best shall be preserved.

No one shall ask for contributions except the servants of the Idean Mother [the goddess Cybele], and they only on appointed days.

Whoever steals or carries off what is sacred or anything entrusted to what is sacred shall be considered as equal in guilt to a parricide.

For the perjurer the punishment from the gods is destruction; the human punishment shall be disgrace.

The pontiffs shall inflict capital punishment on those guilty of incest.

No wicked man shall dare to appease the wrath of the gods with gifts.

Vows shall be scrupulously performed; there shall be a penalty for the violation of the law.

No one shall consecrate a field; the consecration of gold, silver, and ivory shall be confined to reasonable limits.

The sacred rites of families shall remain forever.

The rights of the gods of the lower world shall be sacred. Kinsfolk who are dead shall be considered gods; the expenditure and mourning for them shall be limited.

Cicero, *Laws*, quoted in Naphtali Lewis and Meyer Reinhold, eds., *Roman Civilization, Sourcebook I: The Republic.* New York: Harper and Row, 1966, pp. 466–68.

Appeasing the Woodland Spirits

The Romans believed that most aspects of nature were inhabited by spirits that needed to be appeased when people invaded their spaces. Farmers, for example, regularly conducted ceremonies to appease spirits of the woodlands and fields. In this excerpt from his On Agriculture, *Cato the Elder (243–149 B.C.) gives advice on how to conduct such ceremonies.*

When thinning a grove of trees, it is essential to observe the following Roman ritual. Sacrifice a pig as a propitiatory offering and repeat the following prayer: "Whether you are a god or goddess to whom this grove is sacred, as it is proper to sacrifice to you a pig as a propitiatory offering for the disturbance of this sacred place, and therefore for these reasons whether I or someone I have appointed performs the sacrifice, provided that it be performed correctly, for this reason, in sacrificing this pig, I pray in good faith that you will be benevolent and well disposed to me, my home, my family and my children. For these reasons therefore be honored by the sacrifice of this pig as a propitiatory offering."

If you wish to plow the cleared land in the grove, offer a second propitiatory sacrifice in the same manner but add these words: "for the sake of doing this work."

Cato the Elder, *On Agriculture,* quoted in Jo-Ann Shelton, ed., *As The Romans Did: A Sourcebook in Roman Social History.* New York: Oxford University Press, 1988, pp. 364–65.

A Spirit for Every Action

The number of divine spirits and forces the Romans recognized was and remains bewildering, as a different spirit was assigned to practically every human and natural action. (However, the average person worshiped only those spirits whose actions touched his own life.) In this passage, the Christian writer Augustine (354–430) tries to mock this host of pagan deities. It should be noted that he inaccurately calls them gods and goddesses, which the Romans saw as more powerful and having human form.

How could I possibly record in one passage of this book all the names of the gods and goddesses which the earlier Romans could scarcely enumerate in the huge volumes in which they separated the particular and specific spirits in the environment into individual and distinct categories? They were not willing to entrust the care of all their land to just one deity, but instead assigned their fields to the goddess Rusina, mountain ridges to the god Jugatinus, hills to the goddess Collatina, and valleys to Vallonia. Nor could they find just one goddess, such as Segetia, to whom they could entrust their grain crops once and for all. Instead, when the seed was sown but still under the ground, they chose to have the goddess Seia in charge of it. But once the plants were above the ground and ripening, they put the goddess Segetia in charge. And then when the grain had been harvested and stored, they entrusted to the goddess Tutilina the task of keeping it safe. Who would not have thought that this Segetia was quite sufficient to care for the grain crop all the way through, from its first sprouts to its ripened ears? That was not, however, enough for men who loved a multitude of gods. . . . So the earlier Romans put Proserpina in charge of germinating seeds, and the god Nodutus in charge of the joints and knots of the stems, and the goddess Volutina in charge of the husks folded over the ears; and when the husks open so that the ears may emerge, the goddess Patelana is in charge. . . .

Everyone posts just one doorman to guard the entrance to his home. And since the doorman is human, he is quite sufficient for this task. However, the earlier Romans assigned three gods to this task: Forculus for the doors, Cardea for the

The Romans also worshiped in private ceremonies in the home. These figurines of gods adorn the altar of a house unearthed in the buried city of Pompeii.

hinges, and Limentinus for the threshold. Thus, Forculus was not capable of guarding both the hinge and the threshold as well as the door.

Augustine, *The City of God,* quoted in Jo-Ann Shelton, ed., *As The Romans Did: A Sourcebook in Roman Social History.* New York: Oxford University Press, 1988, pp. 365–66.

Shrine of a River God

The Romans erected shrines to most of the gods and spirits they worshiped. Some were full-blown temples, while others consisted of statues and/or small sanctuaries set up in the areas inhabited by these deities. For example, Pliny the Younger gives this description of the modest but picturesque shrine of the god of a local river. (A common belief was that if such a deity was not appeased, the river might cease to flow.)

Have you ever seen the source of the Clitumnus [a river in Umbria, in north-central Italy]? If not (and I fancy not, or you would have told me) do visit it as I did the other day. I am only sorry I put off seeing it so long.

There is a fair-sized hill which is densely wooded with ancient cypresses; at the foot of this the spring rises and gushes out through several channels of different size, and when its eddies have subsided it broadens out into a pool as clear as glass. . . .

The banks are clothed with ash trees and poplars, whose green reflections can be counted in the clear stream as if they were planted there. The water is as cold and as sparkling as snow. Close by is a holy temple of great antiquity in which is a standing image of the god Clitumnus himself clad in a magistrate's bordered robe; the written oracles lying there prove the presence and prophetic powers of his divinity. All round are a number of small shrines, each containing its god and having its own name and cult, and some of them also their own springs, for as well as the parent stream there are smaller ones which have separate sources but afterwards join the river. The bridge which spans it marks the sacred water off from the ordinary stream: above the bridge boats only are allowed, while below bathing is also permitted. The people of Hispellum, to whom the deified Emperor Augustus presented the site, maintain a bathing place at the town's expense and also provide an inn; and there are several houses picturesquely situated along the river bank. Everything in fact will delight you, and you can also find something to read: you can study the numerous inscriptions in honour of the spring and the god which many hands have written on every pillar and wall. Most of them you will admire, but some will make you laugh—though I know you are really too charitable to laugh at any of them.

Pliny the Younger, *Letters*, published as *The Letters of the Younger Pliny*, trans. Betty Radice. New York: Penguin Books, 1969, pp. 216–17.

Public Sacrifice

One of the pillars of Roman worship was sacrifice, or offering gifts to the gods. In animal sacrifices, the creatures were led to altars to be slaughtered, actions that occurred amid considerable formal ceremony. Here, Livy describes the stately and colorful procession leading up to the sacrifice of two cows to the goddess Juno.

Priests and their attendants lead a bull toward the altar where it will be slaughtered.

A day was immediately proclaimed by the decemvirs [committee in charge of organizing public sacrifice] for another sacrifice to the same goddess. The order of the ceremony was as follows: from the temple of Apollo two white cows were led into the city through the Porta Carmentalis [gate]; behind them were carried two images, in cypress wood, of Queen Juno; then twenty-seven virgins in long robes followed, singing a hymn to Juno. The words of the hymn were no doubt good enough for those rude and uncultivated days, but if I were to quote them now they would sound unpleasing and graceless. The virgins were followed by the decemvirs wearing laurel wreaths and togas with a purple border. The procession passed from the gate by way of the Vicus Jugarius to the forum; there it halted, and the virgins, all taking hold of a rope, moved forward again keeping time with the rhythm of their hymn. From the forum the procession went along the Vicus Tuscus, past the Velabrum and through the cattle-market, and up the Publician hill to the temple of Queen Juno, where the two cows were offered in sacrifice by the decemvirs and the cypress images were taken inside.

Livy, *The History of Rome from Its Foundation*, Books 21–30 published as *Livy: The War with Hannibal*, trans. Aubrey de Sélincourt. New York: Penguin, 1972, pp. 37–38.

A Religious Festival Promotes Fertility

The Romans celebrated numerous annual religious festivals, some to honor specific gods,

others to promote fertility (both agricultural and human). The Lupercalia, celebrated in mid-February, for example, encouraged fertility as well as purified the participants. While attempting to trace the festival's obscure origins in his biography of Romulus, Plutarch provides a valuable description of the rites.

The Lupercalia, by the time of its celebration, may seem to be a feast of purification, for it is solemnised on the *dies nefasti*, or

During the Lupercalia festival, young men strike women with whips to make them fertile.

non court days, of the month February, which name signifies purification, and the very day of the feast was anciently called Februata; but its name is equivalent to the Greek Lycaea; and it seems thus to be of great antiquity. . . . It may come . . . from the wolf that nursed Romulus; and we see the Luperci, the priests, begin their course from the place where they say Romulus was exposed. But the ceremonies performed in it render the origin of the thing more difficult to be guessed at; for there are goats killed, then, two young noblemen's sons being brought, some are to stain their foreheads with the bloody knife, others presently to wipe it off with wool dipped in milk; then the young boys must laugh after their foreheads are wiped; that done, having cut the goats' skins into thongs, they run about naked, only with something about their middle, lashing all they meet; and the young wives do not avoid their strokes, fancying they will help conception and childbirth. Another thing peculiar to this feast is for the Luperci to sacrifice a dog. But, as a certain poet who wrote fabulous explanations of Roman customs in elegiac verses, says, that Romulus and Remus, after the conquest of Amulius, ran joyfully to the place where the wolf gave them suck; and that, in imitation of that, this feast was held, and two young noblemen ran—

> Striking at all, as when from Alba town,
> With sword in hand, the twins came hurrying down;

and that the bloody knife applied to their foreheads was a sign of the danger and bloodshed of that day; the cleansing of them in milk, a remembrance of their food and nourishment. Caius Acilius writes, that, before the city was built, the cattle of Romulus and Remus one day going astray, they, praying to the god Faunus, ran out to seek them naked, wishing not to be troubled with sweat, and that this is why the Luperci run naked. If the sacrifice be by way of purification, a dog might very well be sacrificed, for the Greeks, in their illustrations, carry out young dogs, and frequently use this ceremony of *periscylacismus*, as they call it. Or if again it is a sacrifice of gratitude to the wolf that nourished and preserved Romulus, there is good reason in killing a dog, as being an enemy to wolves. Unless, indeed, after all, the creature is punished for hindering the Luperci in their running.

Plutarch, *Life of Romulus*, in *Parallel Lives*, published complete as *Lives of the Noble Grecians and Romans*, trans. John Dryden. New York: Random House, 1932, pp. 39–40.

Qualifications for Priestesses

Rome's state religion had a number of cults, each cult consisting of the temple, priests (or priestesses), and worship of a particular god. Among the most important and revered was the cult of Vesta, goddess of the hearth. The special priestesses attached to the cult were known as the Vestal Virgins, whose qualifications for the post were listed by the second-century A.D. Roman writer Aulus Gellius.

A Vestal Virgin tends to the fire in the state hearth. These priestesses enjoyed numerous privileges.

It is unlawful for a girl to be chosen who is less than six or more than ten years old; she must also have both father and mother living; she must be free too from any impediment in her speech, must not have impaired hearing, or be marked by any other bodily defect; she must not herself have been freed from parental control, nor

her father before her, even if her father is still living and she is under the control of her grandfather; neither one nor both of her parents may have been slaves or engaged in mean occupations. . . .

Now as soon as the Vestal Virgin is chosen, escorted to the House of Vesta and delivered to the pontiffs [state priests], she immediately passes from the control of her father, without the ceremony of emancipation or loss of civil rights, and acquires the right to make a will. . . .

Now the Vestal is said to be "taken," it appears, because she is grasped by the hand of the chief pontiff and led away from the parent under whose control she is, as if she had been taken in war. In the first book of Fabius Pictor's *History* the formula is given which the chief pontiff should use in taking a Vestal: "I take thee, Amata, as one who has fulfilled all the legal requirements, to be priestess of Vesta, to perform the rites which it is lawful for a Vestal to perform for the Roman people, the Quirites."

Aulus Gellius, *Attic Nights,* quoted in Naphtali Lewis and Meyer Reinhold, eds., *Roman Civilization, Sourcebook I: The Republic.* New York: Harper and Row, 1966, p. 136.

Duties and Powers of the Vestals

In his biography of the legendary Roman king Numa Pompilius, Plutarch gives this illuminating information about the duties and powers of the Vestal Virgins. He also describes their sad and gruesome punishment for breaking their vow of chastity.

The statutes prescribed by Numa for the vestals were these: that they should take a vow of virginity for the space of thirty years, the first ten of which they were to spend in learning their duties, the second ten in performing them, and the remaining ten in teaching and instructing others. Thus the whole term being completed, it was lawful for them to marry, and, leaving the sacred order, to choose any condition of life that pleased them; but this permission few, as they say, made use of; and in cases where they did so, it was observed that their change was not a happy one, but accompanied ever after with regret and melancholy; so that the greater number, from religious fears and scruples, forbore, and continued to old age and death in the strict observance of a single life.

For this condition he compensated by great privileges and prerogatives; as that they had power to make a will in the lifetime of their father; that they had a free administration of their own affairs without guardian or tutor, which was the privilege of women who were the mothers of three children; when they go abroad, they have the fasces [symbols of Roman power] carried before them; and if in their walks they chance to meet a criminal on his way to execution, it saves his life, upon oath made that the meeting was an accidental one, and not concerted or of set purpose. Any one who presses upon the chair on which they are carried, is put to death. If these vestals commit any minor fault, they are punishable by the high priest only, who scourges

the offender, sometimes with her clothes off, in a dark place, with a curtain drawn between; but she that has broken her vow is buried alive near the gate called Collina, where a little mound of earth stands, inside the city, reaching some little distance, called in Latin *agger;* under it a narrow room is constructed, to which a descent is made by stairs; here they prepare a bed, and light a lamp, and leave a small quantity of victuals, such as bread, water, a pail of milk, and some oil; that so that body which had been consecrated and devoted to the most sacred

A Vestal who broke her vow of chastity is sealed in an underground chamber and left to die.

service of religion might not be said to perish by such a death as famine. The culprit herself is put in a litter, which they cover over, and tie her down with cords on it, so that nothing she utters may be heard. They then take her to the forum; all people silently go out of the way as she passes, and such as follow accompany the bier with solemn and speechless sorrow; and indeed, there is not any spectacle more appalling, nor any day observed by the city with greater appearance of gloom and sadness. When they come to the place of execution, the officers loose the cords, and then the high priest, lifting his hands to heaven, pronounces certain prayers to himself before the act; then he brings out the prisoner, being still covered, and placing her upon the steps that lead down to the cell, turns away his face with the rest of the priests; the stairs are drawn up after she has gone down, and a quantity of earth is heaped up over the entrance to the cell, so as to prevent it from being distinguish from the rest of the mound. This is the punishment of those who break their vow of virginity.

Plutarch, *Life of Numa Pompilius*, in *Parallel Lives*, published complete as *Lives of the Noble Grecians and Romans*, trans. John Dryden. New York: Random House, 1932, pp. 82–83.

Formula for Welcoming New Gods

Unusually tolerant in religious matters, the Romans welcomed the gods of their conquered enemies into the Roman fold. The

early fifth-century Roman writer Macrobius mentions this formula, to be recited by the Roman commander on taking possession of the god's sanctuary. (The use of "Carthage" is only an example; the name of any other city or nation could be substituted.)

Whether you are a god or a goddess who hold under your protection the people and city of Carthage, and you also, almighty god, who have taken under your protection this city and this people, to you I pray, you I implore, you I respectfully ask to abandon the people and city of Carthage, to desert their structures, temples, sanctuaries, and urban area, and to leave them. I ask you to instill in that people and city fear, terror, and oblivion, and to come to me [the Roman Commander reciting the vow] and my people when you have left these. I ask that our structures, temples, sanctuaries, and urban area may be more acceptable and more agreeable to you, and that you may take under your protection me and the people of Rome and my soldiers in such a way that we may know and perceive it. If you will do this, I vow that I will build for you temples and celebrate for you games.

Macrobius, *Saturnalia*, quoted in Jo-Ann Shelton, ed., *As The Romans Did: A Sourcebook in Roman Social History.* New York: Oxford University Press, 1988, pp. 369–70.

A Greek God Comes to Rome

During Rome's early centuries, the state began associating various ancient Roman

A statue of Aesculapius, god of healing, whom the Romans imported from Greece.

The Romans on account of a pestilence, at the instructions of the Sibylline books, sent ten envoys under the leadership of Quintus Ogulnius to bring Aesculapius from Epidaurus. When they had arrived there and were marveling at the huge statue of the god, a serpent glided from the temple, an object of veneration rather than of horror, and to the astonishment of all made its way through the midst of the city to the Roman ship, and curled itself up in the tent of Ogulnius. The envoys sailed to Antium, carrying the god, where through the calm sea the serpent made its way to a nearby temple of Aesculapius, and after a few days returned to the ship. And when the ship was sailing up the Tiber, the serpent leaped on the nearby island, where a temple was established to him. The pestilence subsided with astonishing speed.

Anonymous, *On Famous Men*, quoted in Naphtali Lewis and Meyer Reinhold, eds., *Roman Civilization, Sourcebook I: The Republic.* New York: Harper and Row, 1966, p. 143.

deities with Greek gods popular with Rome's Italian neighbors, so that the old Roman agricultural god Mars became synonymous with the Greek god of war, Ares. The first deity imported directly from Greece by the Romans was the healing god Asclepius (whom Rome knew as Aesculapius) in 293 B.C. This short passage from an anonymous work ascribes miraculous effects to the transfer to Rome of a statue of Asclepius.

Worshiping Isis

Another foreign deity the Romans imported was Isis, from Egypt, seen as a mother figure, guardian of the family unit, and bringer of fertility. She had two major yearly festivals, including the Launching of the Ship, which took place on March 5 to celebrate the renewal of life in the spring. In his Golden Ass, *Apuleius describes the festival's rituals through the eyes of his main character (a young man who has been turned into an ass through the workings of black magic).*

I then took my place in the sacred procession and walked along, keeping close attendance on the sacred shrine. I was recognized, indeed I was the cynosure [center of attention] of all eyes; the whole community singled me out with pointing fingers and nods, and gossiped about me: 'Today the venerable power of the almighty goddess has restored him to the ranks of men. How happy, how blessed three times over he is! Doubtless through the purity and faith of his former life he has deserved such sovereign protection from heaven, and in consequence he had been in a manner reborn, and has at once pledged himself to the service of her cult.'

Meanwhile amid the din of joyous prayers we edged our way slowly forward and drew near to the sea-shore, at that very place where as Lucius-turned-ass I had bivouacked [camped out] the previous day. There the gods' statues were duly set in place, and the chief priest named and consecrated to the goddess a ship which had been built with splendid craftsmanship, and which was adorned on all its timbers with wonderful Egyptian pictures. Holding a flaming torch, he first pronounced most solemn prayers from his chaste lips, and then with an egg and sulphur he performed over it an elaborate ceremony of purification. The bright sail of this blessed craft carried upon it woven letters in gold, bearing those same petitions for trouble-free sailing on its first journeys. The mast was of rounded pine, gloriously tall and easily recognized with its striking masthead. The stern was curved in the shape of a goose, and gleamed with its covering of gold leaf. In fact the whole ship shone, polished as it was in clear citrus-wood.

Then the entire population, devotees and uninitiated alike, vied in piling the ship high with baskets laden with spices and similar offerings, and they poured on the waves

A statue of the popular goddess Isis holds a horn of plenty, symbolizing fertility.

libations of meal soaked in milk. Eventually the ship, filled with generous gifts and propitious offerings, was loosed from its anchorropes and launched on the sea before a friendly, specially appointed breeze. Once its progress had caused it to fade from our sight, the bearers of the sacred objects took up again those which each had brought, and they made their eager way back to the temple, following in tidy order the same detail of procession as before.

Once we reached the temple itself, the chief priest, those who carried the gods' images, and those previously initiated into the august inner sanctuary were admitted into the chamber of the goddess, where they duly set in place the living statues. Then one of the company, whom they all termed the scribe, stood before the entrance and summoned an assembly of the *pastophori*; this is the name of the sacred college. There from a high dais [platform] he first recited from a book formulaic prayers for the prosperity of the great emperor, the senate, the knights, and the entire Roman people; then for sea-travellers and for ships journeying within the bounds of our imperial world. Next he announced in the Greek language and according to Greek ritual the ceremony of the launching of the ships. The applause of the people that followed showed that this speech was well received by all. Then the folk, ecstatic with joy, brought up boughs, branches and garlands, and having kissed the feet of the goddess (her statue, wrought from silver, was attached to the temple-steps), they departed to their homes. But my enthusiasm did not permit me to separate myself by more than a nail's breadth from that spot, and I gazed intently on the image of the goddess as I pondered my earlier misfortunes.

Apuleius, *The Golden Ass*, trans. P.G. Walsh. Oxford: Oxford University Press, 1994, pp. 228–29.

A Christian Defends His Faith

One new faith the Romans did not immediately embrace was Christianity. This was not because the Christians worshiped a different god, but rather because they rejected all other gods, refused to recognize the divinity of the emperor, and came under suspicion of committing horrible crimes in their secret rituals. The second-century Christian writer Tertullian defended his faith, suggesting that its bad reputation was based on ignorance.

This then, is the first grievance we lodge against you, the injustice of the hatred you have for the name of Christian. The motive which appears to excuse this injustice is precisely that which both aggravates and convicts it; namely, ignorance. For, what is more unjust than that men should hate what they do not know, even though the matter itself deserves hatred? Only when one knows whether a thing deserves hatred does it deserve it. . . .

For example, evil-doers are anxious to remain in hiding. They shun the light. They tremble when caught; they deny when accused. Even under torture they do not easily or always confess. When condemned beyond all hope, they lament. They tell of the attacks upon themselves of an evil spirit; their moral weaknesses they impute to fate or to the stars. What they recognize as evil they do not want to acknowledge as their own.

In what respect is the Christian like this? No one of them is ashamed, no one has any regrets, except that he was not a Christian earlier. If a charge is brought against him, he glories in it. If he is accused, he offers no defense. When questioned, he confesses of his own accord. For the word of condemnation he gives thanks.

What kind of evil is this that has none of the natural signs of evil—fear, shame, subterfuge, repentance, lament? What crime is this for which the accused rejoices, when the accusation is the object of his prayer and the condemnation his joy? *You* cannot call this madness, you who stand convicted of knowing nothing about it.

If, then, it is decided that we are the most wicked of men, why do you treat us so differently from those who are on a par with us, that is, from all other criminals? The same treatment ought to be meted out for the same crime.

When others are charged with the same crimes as we, they use their own lips and the hired eloquence of others to prove their innocence. There is full liberty given to answer the charge and to cross-question, since it is unlawful for men to be condemned without defense or without a hearing. Christians alone are permitted to say nothing that would clear their name, vindi-

cate the truth, and aid the judge to come to a fair decision. One thing only is what they wait for; this is the only thing necessary to arouse public hatred: the confession of the name of Christian, not an investigation of the charge.

Tertullian, *Apology*, quoted in William G. Sinnigen, ed., *Sources in Western Civilization: Rome.* New York: Free Press, 1965, pp. 198–200.

The Edict of Milan Grants Toleration to Christians

Despite the efforts of Christian apologists like Tertullian, the Roman government continued to distrust the faith and periodically launched persecutions against it. The situation improved markedly for the Christians after 313, when the emperors Constantine and Licinius granted them toleration in the so-called Edict of Milan, excerpted here.

We, Constantinus and Licinius the Emperors, having met in concord at Milan and having set in order everything which pertains to the common good and public security, are of the opinion that among the various things which we perceived would profit men, or which should be set in order first, was to be found the cultivation of religion; we should therefore give both to Christians and to all others free facility to follow the religion which each may desire, so that by this means whatever divinity is enthroned in heaven may be gracious and favourable to us and to all who have been placed under our authority. Therefore we are of the opinion that the following decision is in accordance with sound and true reasoning: that no one who has given his mental assent to the Christian persuasion or to any other which he feels to be suitable to him should be compelled to deny his conviction, so that the Supreme Godhead ("Summa Divinitas"), whose worship we freely observe, can assist us in all things with his wonted favour and benevolence. Wherefore it is necessary for your Excellency to know that it is our pleasure that all restrictions which were previous-

A Roman pagan is baptized, marking his conversion to Christianity.

ly put forward in official pronouncements concerning the sect of the Christians should be removed, and that each one of them who freely and sincerely carries out the purpose of observing the Christian religion may endeavour to practise its precepts without any fear or danger. We believed that these points should be fully brought to your attention, so that you might know that we have given free and absolute permission to practise their religion to the Christians. Now that you perceive what we have granted to them, your Excellency must also learn that for the sake of peace in our time a similar public and free right to practise their religion or cult is granted to others, so that every man may have free opportunity to worship according to his own wish. This has been done by us to avoid any appearance of disfavour to any one religion.

Constantine and Licinius, *Edict of Milan*, quoted in Brian Tierney, ed., *The Middle Ages: Volume I, Sources of Medieval History.* New York: Knopf, 1973, pp. 21–22.

A Losing Fight to Retain Traditional Worship

Only a few decades after the Edict of Milan, Christian leaders managed to make Christianity the official religion of Rome, supplanting the traditional gods and cults. Many pagans objected, however. A notable case occurred in 384 when the government, urged on by the influential Christian bishop Ambrose, removed the statue of the goddess Victory from the Senate House; as shown in the following excerpts, the noted pagan writer

Symmachus lodged a formal complaint and Ambrose answered it. Eventually, Ambrose prevailed, the pagans continued to lose ground, and within a few more generations almost all the inhabitants of Europe were Christian.

Symmachus:

It is our task to watch on behalf of your Graces. The glory of these times makes it suitable that we defend the institutions of our ancestors and the rights and destiny of our country. That glory is all the greater when you understand that you may not do anything contrary to the custom of your ancestors. We demand then the restoration of that condition of religious affairs which was so long advantageous to the state. . . .

The divine Mind has distributed different guardians and different cults to different cities. As souls are separately given to infants as they are born, so to peoples the genius of their destiny. Here comes in the proof from advantage, which most of all vouches to man for the gods. For, since our reason is wholly clouded, whence does the knowledge of the gods more rightly come to us, than from the memory and evidence of prosperity? Now if a long period gives authority to religious customs, we ought to keep faith with so many centuries, and to follow our ancestors, as they happily followed theirs. . . .

We ask, then, for peace for the gods of our fathers and of our country. It is just that all worship should be considered as one. We look on the same stars, the sky is common, the same world surrounds us. What difference does it make by what pains each seeks the truth? We cannot attain to so great a secret by one road; but this discussion is rather for persons at ease, we offer now prayers, not conflict . . .

Ambrose:

The illustrious Prefect of the city [i.e., Symmachus] . . . complains with sad and tearful words, asking, as he says, for the restoration of the rites of her ancient ceremonies. . . .

Your sacrifice is a rite of being sprinkled with the blood of beasts. Why do you seek the voice of God in dead animals? Come and learn on earth the heavenly warfare; we live here, but our warfare is there. Let God Himself, Who made me, teach me the mystery of heaven, not man, who knew not himself. Whom rather than God should I believe concerning God? How can I believe you, who confess that you know not what you worship?

By one road, says he, one cannot attain to so great a secret. What you know not, that we know by the voice of God. And what you seek by fancies, we have found out from the very Wisdom and Truth of God. Your ways, therefore, do not agree with ours. You implore peace for your gods from the Emperors, we ask for peace for the Emperors themselves from Christ. You worship the works of your own hands, we think it an offence that anything which can be made should be esteemed God. God wills not that He should be worshipped in stones.

Quoted in Brian Tierney, ed., *The Middle Ages: Volume I, Sources of Medieval History.* New York: Knopf, 1973, pp. 23–26.

Chronology of Ancient Rome

B.C.

ca. 1000 (and probably much earlier)
Latin tribesmen establish small villages on some of the seven hills marking the site of the future city of Rome.

753
Traditional founding date for the city of Rome by Romulus (as computed and accepted by Roman scholars some seven centuries later).

753–717
Supposed years of Romulus's reign as Rome's first king.

534–509
Supposed years of the reign of Tarquinius Superbus, Rome's last king.

509
The leading Roman landowners throw out their last king and establish the Roman Republic.

496
The Romans defeat the other members of the Latin League at Lake Regillus.

ca. 451–450
The Twelve Tables, Rome's first law code, are inscribed and adopted.

445
The Romans pass a law allowing patricians (aristocrats) and plebeians (commoners) to marry one another.

396
After a long siege, the Romans capture the important Etruscan town of Veii.

390
At the Allia River, a Roman army suffers a major defeat at the hands of a force of invading Gauls, who proceed to sack Rome.

366
The first plebeian consul is elected.

343–341
The First Samnite War, fought in the Campania (south of Rome).

340–338
Rome defeats the Latin League, dissolves it, and incorporates the territories of some of its members into the growing Roman state.

321
During the Second Samnite War, a Roman army surrenders to a force of Samnites at the Caudine Forks.

312
The building of Rome's first major road, the Appian Way, and its first aqueduct, the Aqua Appia.

ca. 300
Rome's high priests begin keeping historical records known as the *Annales Maximi;* the Greek thinker Zeno founds the Stoic philosophical movement, which in succeeding

years will become extremely popular among Roman intellectuals.

ca. 289
Rome mints its first coins.

280–275
The Romans fight several battles with the Greek Hellenistic king Pyrrhus, who has come to the aid of the Greek cities of southern Italy; his victories are so costly that he abandons the Italian Greeks to their fate.

265
Having gained control of the Italian Greek cities, Rome is master of the entire Italian peninsula.

264–241
The First Punic War, in which Rome defeats the maritime empire of Carthage.

218–201
Rome fights Carthage again in the Second Punic War, in which the Carthaginian general Hannibal crosses the Alps, invades Italy, and delivers the Romans one crippling defeat after another.

216
Hannibal crushes a large Roman army at Cannae (in southeastern Italy); Roman fatalities exceed fifty thousand.

202
After the Romans weather the storm and rebound, their greatest general, Scipio Africanus, defeats Hannibal on the plain of Zama (in North Africa).

200–197
The Romans defeat Macedonia in the Second Macedonian War.

190
A Roman army defeats the Seleucid king Antiochus III at Magnesia (in Asia Minor).

168
The Third Macedonian War comes to a close as the Romans defeat Macedonia's King Perseus; the Macedonian kingdom is dismantled.

153
The Romans change the first month of their year from March to January.

149–146
Rome annihilates Carthage in the Third Punic War.

135–132
The Romans put down a large slave rebellion in Sicily.

133
Death of the social reformer Tiberius Sempronius Gracchus.

112–105
Rome fights and defeats a North African prince, Jugurtha.

107
The Roman general Marius, who will soon initiate important military reforms, wins the first of his several consulships.

102
Marius defeat the Teutones, a large Germanic tribe that has invaded Gaul and threatens northern Italy.

100
Birth of Julius Caesar, one of the greatest statesmen and military generals in history.

90–88
The Social War, in which many of Rome's Italian allies resort to violence to acquire full citizenship.

88–82
A civil war rages between the supporters of Marius and Sulla.

ca. 80
The first all-stone Roman amphitheater opens in the town of Pompeii.

74–63
Rome defeats Mithridates VI of Pontus in the Third Mithridatic War.

73–71
The Thracian slave Spartacus leads the last of Rome's large slave rebellions; the Roman nobleman Marcus Crassus eventually defeats the slaves.

67
The noted general Pompey rids the Mediterranean sea lanes of pirates in only forty days, becoming a national hero.

65
Caesar stages the first large public gladiatorial combats in Rome.

63
The senator/consul Cicero exposes a plot by the disgruntled nobleman Catiline to topple the government.

60
Caesar, Pompey, and Crassus form a strong political alliance later referred to as the First Triumvirate.

58
The Theater of Pompey, seating some eighty thousand people, opens in Rome.

58–51
Caesar conquers the peoples of Transalpine Gaul.

53
Crassus is defeated and killed by the Parthians at Carrhae, in the Near East.

49
Caesar crosses the Rubicon River, initiating a new civil war; the following year he defeats Pompey at Pharsalus (in Greece).

46
Caesar defeats some of Pompey's supporters at Thapsus (in North Africa).

44
After declaring himself "dictator for life," Caesar is assassinated by a group of senators; Cicero completes his great work dealing with moral philosophy, *On Duties.*

43
Caesar's associate, Antony; Caesar's adopted son, Octavian; and a powerful general, Lepidus, establish the Second Triumvirate; they proceed to murder their political enemies, including Cicero, the last great republican champion.

42
Antony and Octavian defeat the leaders of the conspiracy against Caesar at Philippi (in northern Greece); at this point, the Republic is effectively dead.

31
Octavian defeats Antony and Egypt's queen Cleopatra at Actium (in western Greece) and gains firm control of the Mediterranean world.

ca. 30 B.C.–A.D. 180
The approximate years of the so-called Pax Romana ("Roman peace"), a period in which the Mediterranean world under the first several Roman emperors enjoys relative peace and prosperity.

29–17
The Roman poet Virgil composes the *Aeneid*, which becomes Rome's national epic.

27
The Senate confers on Octavian the name of Augustus (the "exalted one"); historians usually mark this date as the beginning of the Roman Empire.

ca. 23
The poet Horace publishes his *Odes*.

20
Augustus sets up a board of curators (the *curatores viarum*) to manage Italy's public highways.

9
Augustus dedicates the *Ara Pacis* (Altar of Peace), one of Rome's architectural master-pieces.

4
Jesus is born in Bethlehem (in the Roman province of Judaea).

2
Augustus dedicates a magnificent new forum, named for himself, in Rome.

A.D.

6
Augustus establishes a fire-fighting force (the *vigiles*) to protect the Roman capital.

9
A Roman army commanded by Publius Quinctilius Varus is annihilated in the Teutoberg Forest (in western Germany); thereafter, the Romans abandon their plans to absorb the German lands.

14
Augustus dies, plunging the Roman people into a period of deep mourning; he is succeeded by Tiberius.

17
Death of the poet Ovid, marking the close of the Augustan Age of literature, Rome's greatest literary period.

20
The first large state-run public bathhouse opens in Rome.

ca. 30–33
Jesus is executed on the orders of Pontius Pilate, the Roman governor of Judaea.

64
A great fire ravages large sections of Rome; the emperor Nero unfairly blames the disaster on the Christians and initiates the first of a series of persecutions against them; he also begins to erect a fabulous new palace for himself, the Golden House.

69
The so-called year of the four emperors, in which several Roman generals vie for supremacy; Vespasian emerges the victor and founds the Flavian dynasty.

70
Titus, Vespasian's son, besieges and captures the Jewish city of Jerusalem.

79
The volcano Mt. Vesuvius erupts, burying the towns of Pompeii and Herculaneum; the great naturalist Pliny the Elder dies while observing the disaster at close range.

80
Titus inaugurates the Colosseum.

98–117
Reign of the emperor Trajan, in which the Roman Empire reaches its greatest size and power.

107
Trajan stages public games lasting 123 days, during which some eleven thousand animals are slaughtered.

ca. 115–117
The distinguished Roman historian Tacitus writes the *Annals*.

ca. 122
The emperor Hadrian visits Britain and plans the construction of the massive defensive wall that will bear his name.

166
The Marcomanni and other Germanic tribes invade Rome's northern border provinces; a terrible plague spreads across the Empire.

180
Death of the emperor Marcus Aurelius, marking the end of the Pax Romana and the beginning of Rome's steady slide into economic and political crisis.

192
The corrupt emperor Commodus is assassinated.

193–235
Period of the combined reigns of the emperors of the Severan dynasty, beginning with Septimius Severus and ending with Severus Alexander.

212
The emperor Caracalla extends citizenship rights to all free adult males in the Empire.

215
Caracalla issues a new coin of silver and bronze, the *antoninianus*.

235–284
The Empire suffers under the strain of terrible political upheaval and civil strife, prompting later historians to call this period "the anarchy."

284
Diocletian ascends the throne and initiates sweeping political, economic, and social reforms, in effect reconstructing the Empire under a new blueprint; modern historians often call this new realm the Later Empire.

293
Diocletian establishes the First Tetrarchy, a power-sharing arrangement in which two emperors (with the title of Augustus) reign, one in the east, the other in the west, each with an assistant (with the title of Caesar).

305
Diocletian abdicates and retires, the first Roman emperor to do so; the Second Tetrarchy he has engineered to replace him soon falls apart as its members and some of their sons begin to fight one another.

306–337
Reign of the emperor Constantine I, who carries on the reforms begun by Diocletian.

312
Constantine defeats his rival, the usurper Maxentius, at Rome's Milvian Bridge.

313
Constantine and his eastern colleague, Licinius, issue the so-called Edict of Milan,

granting religious toleration to the formerly hated and persecuted Christians.

330

Constantine founds the city of Constantinople, on the Bosporus Strait, making it the capital of the eastern section of the Empire.

337

Constantine dies; he converts to Christianity on his deathbed.

361–363

Reign of the emperor Julian, who, in face of Christianity's growing popularity, tries but fails to reestablish paganism as Rome's dominant religion.

ca. 370

The Huns, a savage nomadic people from central Asia, sweep into eastern Europe, pushing the Goths and other "barbarian" peoples into the northern Roman provinces.

374

The Roman state passes a law banning the exposure of unwanted infants.

378

The eastern emperor Valens is disastrously defeated by the Visigoths and Ostrogoths at Adrianople (in Thrace).

391

At the urgings of Christian leaders, especially the bishop Ambrose, the emperor Theodosius I closes the pagan temples, demolishing some and turning others into museums.

395

Theodosius dies, leaving his sons Arcadius and Honorius in control of a permanently divided Roman realm.

ca. 407

As Rome steadily loses control of several of its northern and western provinces, Britain falls under the sway of barbarian tribes.

410

The Visigoths, led by Alaric, sack Rome.

426

The great Roman Christian thinker and writer Augustine completes his monumental *City of God*.

438

The eastern emperor Theodosius II completes the Theodosian Code, a systematic, sixteen-volume large compilation of Roman laws.

451

After terrorizing and pillaging Roman lands for more than a decade, Attila, war chief of the Huns, is defeated by a combined army of Romans and barbarian federates at Chalons, in what is now northern France.

455

Rome is sacked again, this time by the Vandals, led by Gaiseric.

476

The German-born general Odoacer demands that the emperor, the young Romulus Augustulus, grant him and his men federate status; when the emperor refuses, Odoacer deposes him and no new emperor takes his place; the succession of Roman emperors continues in the eastern realm, which steadily evolves into the Byzantine Empire.

Index

Picture Credits

Cover Photo: © Araldo de Luca/
   CORBIS
©Araldo de Luca/CORBIS, 70, 75
©The Art Archive/Picture-desk, 74,
   86, 91, 101, 108, 115
©Bettmann/CORBIS, 17, 29, 42, 111
©Hulton Archive/Getty Images, 27,
   31, 60, 94

Joseph Paris Picture Archives, 34, 52,
   55, 64, 67, 69, 80, 82, 83, 85, 87,
   93, 99, 104, 105, 112
Mary Evans Picture Library, 9, 12, 13,
   22, 46, 57, 106, 109
North Wind Picture Archives, 15, 44,
   49, 72, 77, 89
Steve Zmina, 33, 38

About the Editor

Classical historian Don Nardo has published many volumes about ancient Roman history and culture, including *The Punic Wars, The Age of Augustus, A Travel Guide to Ancient Rome, Life of a Roman Gladiator, Greek and Roman Science,* and Greenhaven Press's massive *Encyclopedia of Greek and Roman Mythology.* Mr. Nardo also writes screenplays and teleplays and composes music. He lives in Massachusetts with his wife, Christine.